Powerful Men

The 25 most powerful men
in modern history

Phillips Tahuer
Ediciones Afrodita

Contents

Introduction
1.   Nelson Mandela
2.   Mahatma Gandhi
3.   Winston Churchill
4.   Franklin D. Roosevelt
5.   Adolf Hitler
6.   Joseph Stalin
7.   Mao Zedong
8.   Martin Luther King Jr.
9.   John F. Kennedy
10. Pablo Picasso
11. Steve Jobs
12. Bill Gates
13. Elon Musk
14. Vladimir Putin
15. Papa Francisco
16. Jeff Bezos
17. Xi Jinping
18. Henry Kissinger
19. Richard Branson
20. Fidel Castro
21. Vladimir Lenin
22. Mark Zuckerberg
23. Karl Marx
24. Sigmund Freud
25. Albert Einstein

Introduction

Concept of power

Power can be defined as the ability to influence, direct, or control the behavior of other people or the course of events. It is a force that can originate from various sources and manifest itself in different ways. In general terms, power implies the ability to affect decisions, change perceptions, and mobilize resources to achieve specific objectives.

It does not in any way refer to the results being good or moral, power is only reflected when it causes effects. It may happen that a person occupies the most important position in a country, but it turns out that, due to having a timid character, the real power is exercised by another in the shadows.

Types of Power: Coercive Power: Based on the ability to impose sanctions or punishments. This type of power is exercised when someone can force others to act in a certain way under threat of negative consequences.

Reward Power: It arises from the ability to offer rewards or incentives. It is based on the promise of benefits in exchange for conformity or performance.

Legitimate Power: This power is derived from an officially recognized position or role within a social, political, or organizational structure. This power is based on the acceptance of established norms and rules.

Expert Power: This power comes from specialized knowledge or technical skills that someone possesses and that others value. People trust those who have specific experience and skills.

Reference Power: This power is based on admiration or respect for a person. This type of power is exercised when others want to imitate or align themselves with the values and behaviors of the person who possesses it.

Information Power: This power is based on the control or access to key information that others do not possess. Those who have crucial information can influence decisions and actions.

Relationship of power with people Power is intrinsically linked to human relationships and can have a profound impact on how these relationships develop and on the structure of society. Some of the ways power relates to people are Social Dynamics: Power determines how resources are distributed, decisions are made, and hierarchies are established within groups and societies. People who hold power have the ability to influence social norms, policies, and the daily lives of people around them.

Influence and Persuasion: Power allows people to persuade and motivate others to act in a certain way. This type of influence can be direct, as in the case of a leader mobilizing his team toward a common goal, or indirect, as in the way public figures shape attitudes and behaviors through the media.

Authority Relationships: In organizational and political contexts, power manifests itself through authority relationships, where those in leadership positions have the ability to make decisions that affect those at lower hierarchical levels. This relationship can foster a sense of obligation and conformity, but it can also generate conflict and resistance.

Inequality and Conflict: Unequal distribution of power can lead to conflict and inequality. When power is concentrated in the hands of a few, it can result in the marginalization of groups and the perpetuation of injustices. Power struggles often reflect tensions between different interests and aspirations.

Empowerment: Power is also related to empowerment, which is the process of increasing the ability of a person or group to control their life and make decisions. Empowerment involves providing people with the resources, knowledge, and support necessary for them to exercise their own power and influence their environment.

Power in the 20th and 21st Centuries: Political, Economic, and Cultural Influence in a Globalized World

In the 21st century, the concept of power has evolved significantly. It is no longer just about territorial or military domination, as it was until the 20th century, but the ability to exert influence is manifested in increasingly broader and more complex spheres: politics, economics, and culture. As the world becomes more interconnected, these forms of power interact and intertwine, shaping the reality of millions of people worldwide.

Political Power: Global Governance and Leadership

Political power has traditionally been a dominant force, but in the modern era, its scope and dynamics have changed. Today's political leaders face the challenge of handling not only national affairs but also international issues that require global collaboration and negotiation. Figures such as Angela Merkel, Vladimir Putin and Xi Jinping have demonstrated how national politics can have a global impact. Merkel, as German chancellor, played a crucial role in European politics and in managing crises such as migration and the COVID-19 pandemic. Putin and Xi, for their part, have reinforced the influence of Russia and China on the world stage, each in their own way, through domestic policies that have international ramifications. The creation of the BRICS is a sign of the new world order that is taking shape.

Furthermore, the ability to influence global policies through international bodies and multilateral agreements is a crucial facet of contemporary political power. The ability of leaders to form coalitions, negotiate treaties, and manage diplomatic relations demonstrates how political power has become a network of global interactions.

Economic Power: Transformation through Capital and Innovation

In the global economy, power manifests itself in the ability to control resources, capital, and technological innovation. Steve Jobs and Bill Gates are emblematic examples of how economic power can transform society. Jobs, with Apple, revolutionized technology and communication, while Gates, with Microsoft, made personal computing accessible worldwide. Both have shaped the way we interact with technology and, therefore, how our economies and lives operate.

Economic power resides not only in individuals and corporations but also in nations and economic alliances. The monetary and fiscal policies of large economies such as the United States, China, and the European Union have significant impacts on global markets, exchange rates, and global economic stability. Dominance in strategic sectors, from energy to technology, demonstrates how economic power can influence global well-being.

Cultural Power: Influence through Media and Ideas

Cultural power has become increasingly relevant in an interconnected world. Through media, entertainment, and the dissemination of ideas, individuals and institutions can shape perceptions, attitudes, and behaviors worldwide. Oprah Winfrey, with her television show and media influence, has had a profound impact on culture and the way issues such as well-being, education and human rights are addressed. Similarly, Bono, with his activism in human rights and global development, has used his platform to promote social and political change.

Cultural influence is also manifested in the globalization of trends and values. The ability to spread ideas and fashions through digital platforms has democratized access to culture, allowing social movements and causes to quickly gain traction around the world. Memes, social media and digital entertainment are now powerful tools for the creation and dissemination of ideas.

Intersections and Challenges

In practice, these three types of power—political, economic, and cultural—do not operate in isolation. They often intertwine and influence each other. For example, political decisions can affect the global economy, and cultural currents can influence public policy. The rise of digital platforms has amplified this intertwining, allowing for an unprecedented interconnection between politics, economics, and culture.

However, this intertwining also presents challenges. The unmeasured influence of individuals or corporations can lead to inequalities and abuses of power. Global policies can be influenced by economic interests that do not always coincide with the common good. And cultural diffusion can sometimes lead to cultural homogenization, to the detriment of local diversity.

Below, we will develop a limited list of men who are generally considered to be the most influential from the 20th century to the present.

The selection of people in this book is largely subjective and depends on the criteria used: Geographical reach of power, duration of impact of their influence, nature of power, methods used, and legitimacy of power.

The list below is based on the ability of these men to influence large sections of society, whether through politics, culture, technology, or religion. Each of them has left a lasting mark on modern history, for better or worse.

1. Nelson Mandela

Nelson Rolihlahla Mandela was born in Mvezo, Umtata, then part of the Cape Colony in South Africa (now part of the Eastern Cape Province) on 18 July 1918, to a family of Thembu ethnicity, a branch of the Xhosa. His name "Rolihlahla" translates as "branch puller" or, more figuratively, "troublemaker". His father, Gadla Henry Mphakanyiswa, was the chief of the Thembu clan, and his mother, Nosekeni Fanny, was a respected woman in the community. Mandela attended primary school in the village of Qunu, where his teacher gave him the name "Nelson", a common practice at the time for African children.

In 1939, Mandela moved to the University of Fort Hare, one of the most important educational institutions for Africans at the time. During his time at university, Mandela became involved in student activism and joined the African Students League, laying the groundwork for his future leadership.

After completing his education at Fort Hare, Mandela moved to Johannesburg, where he joined the African National Congress (ANC) political party in 1943. In 1944, along with other young leaders, he founded the ANC Youth League, which promoted a more radical vision for the fight against apartheid, a system of institutionalized racial segregation and discrimination in South Africa.

In 1952, Mandela and Oliver Tambo founded the first black-owned law firm in South Africa, providing legal assistance to those who could not afford to pay. The ANC's civil disobedience strategy was a central focus during the 1950s and 1960s, and Mandela became a prominent figure in the fight against the apartheid regime.

On 5 August 1962, Mandela was arrested and, following a trial in 1964, was sentenced to life imprisonment for sabotage and conspiracy to overthrow the government. He spent 27 years in prison, mostly on Robben Island, where his spirit and leadership became international symbols of the struggle for justice and equality.

In 1990, Nelson Mandela was released from prison, marking the beginning of a new era in South Africa. His release was the result of a growing international anti-apartheid movement and internal pressure within the country. From then on, Mandela led negotiations for the end of apartheid and the transition to a multiracial democracy.

In 1991, Mandela was elected president of the ANC at its national conference in Durban, and in 1993 he was awarded the Nobel Peace Prize jointly with then South African President F.W. de Klerk for their efforts in reconciliation and negotiating the end of apartheid.

On April 27, 1994, South Africa held its first democratic elections and Nelson Mandela became the country's first black president. His presidency focused on national reconciliation, the establishment of a Truth and Reconciliation Commission (chaired by Desmond Tutu), and the implementation of policies to improve the lives of disadvantaged South Africans.

After his presidency, Mandela retired from active political life in 1999 but continued to work on various humanitarian and philanthropic causes. He founded the Nelson Mandela Foundation, which focused on education, health, and community development. He also played an active role in promoting peace and human rights globally.

The political leader passed away on December 5, 2013, in Johannesburg, South Africa.

His legacy is vast and multidimensional. His fight against apartheid, his ability to reconcile a divided nation, and his commitment to social justice have left an indelible mark on world history. Mandela became a symbol of peaceful resistance and the power of forgiveness.

The impact of his actions was so profound that his figure has become a model for leaders and activists around the world. In 2013, his passing was an event of great international significance, with world leaders and citizens around the globe paying tribute to his life and work.

Nelson Mandela not only fought against an oppressive system, but also demonstrated that the power of perseverance, peace, and dialogue can overcome the toughest barriers. His life and legacy continue to inspire generations in the search for justice, equality, and reconciliation.

2. Mahatma Gandhi

Mohandas Karamchand Gandhi was born on October 2, 1869, in Porbandar, Kathiawar State, British India (now Gujarat, India). Known worldwide as Mahatma Gandhi, he was raised in a family of the Vaishya merchant community in Porbandar, a coastal city in the state of Gujarat. His father, Karamchand Gandhi, was the diwan (chief minister) of Porbandar State, and his mother, Putlibai, was known for her religious devotion.

Gandhi received a traditional Indian education in primary and secondary school, and in 1888 he traveled to London to study law at University College London. During his time in England, Gandhi committed himself to a life of simplicity and began to become acquainted with the ideas of thinkers such as Henry David Thoreau and Leo Tolstoy, whose concepts influenced his future philosophy of nonviolent resistance.

In 1893, Gandhi moved to South Africa to work as a lawyer on a racial discrimination case. During his 21-year stay in South Africa, he experienced first-hand racism and injustice against the Indian community. It was in this context that he developed and refined his approach of "Satyagraha" or non-violent resistance, relying on truth and non-violence as tools of protest and social change.

Gandhi organized several campaigns for equal rights for Indians in South Africa, including protests registration laws that required Indians to carry identification. His innovative approach to non-violent resistance and civil disobedience enabled him to win significant victories in South Africa and laid the groundwork for his future struggle in India.

Gandhi returned to India in 1915 and quickly became a central figure in the independence movement. His philosophy of non-violent resistance and methods of peaceful protest captured the imagination of the Indian people and won the support of the masses.

In 1919, Gandhi organized a mass civil disobedience campaign against the Rowlatt Act, a law that allowed British authorities to arrest and detain people without trial. The campaign was a significant success, but it was also marked by the violence that erupted in the Amritsar riot of 1919, where hundreds of Indians were killed by British soldiers. Gandhi responded with a call for a general strike and a boycott of British goods.

In 1930, Gandhi launched the famous Salt March, a 240-mile protest the British monopoly on salt production. The march attracted international attention and strengthened the position of the Indian National Congress as the leading force in the struggle for independence.

Gandhi's Non-Cooperation Movement, launched in 1920, was a nationwide protest British rule that included boycotts of British institutions, courts, and products. Although the movement faced challenges and periods of repression, Gandhi's campaign helped mobilize millions of Indians around the cause of independence.

The Salt March was a dramatic demonstration of the power of nonviolent resistance. Gandhi and his followers marched from their ashram in Sabarmati to the Dandi coast to produce salt in violation of British law. This symbolic act of disobedience attracted worldwide attention and underlined the injustice of colonial rule.

In 1942, Gandhi launched the "Do or Die" (Quit India) Campaign, demanding an immediate end to British rule. The campaign was widely suppressed, and Gandhi and other Congress leaders were arrested. Despite this, the pressure of nonviolent resistance campaigns and the increasing tension of World War II led the British to reconsider their position.

India's independence was finally realized on August 15, 1947, when India broke free from British rule. However, the partition of the country into India and Pakistan, which was a source of great pain and violence, was a cause of great sadness for Gandhi, who had advocated for a united and harmonious India.

Gandhi continued to work for peace and reconciliation between Hindus and Muslims until his assassination on January 30, 1948, by Nathuram Godse, a Hindu extremist who opposed his peace efforts. The news of his death shocked the entire world, and his funeral became a global event of mourning.

Gandhi's legacy is deeply influential globally. His approach to nonviolent resistance and simple philosophy of life inspired civil rights and liberation movements around the world. Leaders such as Martin Luther King Jr., Nelson Mandela, and Cesar Chavez have cited Gandhi as a crucial influence in their struggles for justice and equality.

Gandhi's impact on global history is manifested in his ability to mobilize millions of people through peaceful methods and his contribution to the creation of an India free from colonial rule. His life and teachings continue to be a beacon of hope and a reminder of the power of peaceful resistance in the pursuit of justice.

Mahatma Gandhi, with his firm belief in non-violence and truth, revolutionized the way people can fight oppression and injustice. His life is a testament to the power of the human spirit to transform reality and bring about lasting change through peaceful means.

3. Winston Churchill

Sir Winston Leonard Spencer-Churchill was born on November 30, 1874, at Blenheim Palace, Oxfordshire, England, as the second son of Lord Randolph Churchill, a prominent Conservative politician, and Lady Randolph Churchill (born Jennie Jerome), an American socialite. From an early age, Churchill was surrounded by the splendour of high society and politics, which influenced his future career.

Churchill attended Harrow Grammar School, where he displayed a rebellious character and academic difficulties. Afterwards, he transferred to the Royal Military Academy Sandhurst, where he studied to become an officer in the British Army. His military career began with a trip to Cuba to cover the Cuban War of Independence as a correspondent and continued with various campaigns in India, Sudan and South Africa, where he participated in the Second Boer War.

Churchill entered politics in 1900 when he was elected Member of Parliament for Oldham as a Conservative. His political career was marked by his ability to change parties, which he did in 1904 when he joined the Liberal Party. During his time with the Liberals, Churchill was appointed Trade Secretary in 1908 and subsequently served as First Lord of the Admiralty in 1911.

In his role as First Lord of the Admiralty, Churchill pushed for the modernisation of the British fleet and fostered the creation of the Royal Naval Air Service. However, his reputation took a hit following the failure of the Dardanelles campaign in World War I, leading to his resignation and a brief retirement from politics.

Following his resignation, Churchill enlisted in the army and served on the front lines of World War I. His experience on the battlefield allowed him to regain his reputation and in 1924 he returned to government as Chancellor of the Exchequer under Conservative Prime Minister Stanley Baldwin. During his tenure, Churchill championed the policy of returning to the gold standard, a decision that had negative economic consequences.

Throughout the 1930s, Churchill was a marginal figure in British politics, but his warnings about the growing power of Nazi Germany and his opposition to appeasing Hitler kept him at the center of political debate.

Churchill's true impact was cemented during the Second World War. In May 1940, following the resignation of Neville Chamberlain, Churchill was appointed Prime Minister. His leadership during the war was crucial, especially in the early years when the United Kingdom faced the imminent danger of a Nazi invasion.

Churchill was noted for his inspirational speeches and his ability to maintain high morale in times of adversity. Quotes such as "Never in the field of human history was so much owed by so many to so few" referred to the Royal Air Force pilots during the Battle of Britain. His ability to galvanize the British people and the Allies was critical to the resistance against the Axis and the eventual Allied triumph.

In 1941, Churchill met with U.S. President Franklin D. Roosevelt at the Atlantic Conference, which laid the groundwork for the U.S.-British alliance and the declaration of common goals in the postwar period.

After victory in World War II, Churchill was defeated in the 1945 general election but continued to play an important role in global politics. In 1946, he gave the famous "Iron Curtain" speech in Fulton, Missouri, warning of the growing power of the Soviet Union and the need for a strong Western alliance.

Churchill returned to power as Prime Minister in 1951 and his second term was marked by foreign policy and the management of decolonization. During this time, he oversaw the decolonization process in Africa and Asia, supporting the independence of several nations.

Winston Churchill left a legacy that transcends his role as a war leader. He was an influential politician, a prolific writer, and a gifted orator. His ability to use language as a tool to inspire and motivate people is one of the most memorable features of his career.

In 1953, Churchill was awarded the Nobel Prize in Literature for his speeches and writings, highlighting his impact on literature and history. His legacy is also reflected in his contributions to international politics and the way he faced the challenge of totalitarianism.

Churchill died on 24 January 1965 at the age of 90 in London, and his state funeral was one of the most extensive in the history of the United Kingdom. His influence lives on in politics, strategy, and communication, and he remains an iconic figure of leadership during times of crisis.

Winston Churchill was a key figure in 20th-century history, whose ability to lead, inspire, and communicate had a profound impact on the course of World War II and global politics. His life and work continue to be studied and admired, and his legacy as a visionary leader and persuasive speaker endures as an example of courage and determination in times of adversity.

4. Franklin D. Roosevelt

Franklin Delano Roosevelt was born on January 30, 1882, in Hyde Park, New York, United States, to a wealthy family. He was the only child of James Roosevelt, a prominent businessman and politician, and Sara Delano Roosevelt, a woman of Dutch descent. The Roosevelt family was well-positioned in New York high society, and Franklin grew up in an environment of privilege and education.

Roosevelt attended Groton School, a prestigious preparatory institution, and then studied at Harvard, graduating in 1903. During his time at Harvard, he developed an interest in politics and international relations and was an editor of the university magazine. His educational background and family environment influenced his later political career.

In 1905, Roosevelt married Eleanor Roosevelt, his distant cousin and an influential figure in his career. Eleanor became a prominent advocate for civil rights and a key figure in politics and social reforms.

After graduating from Harvard, Roosevelt attended Columbia University to study law, although he did not complete his legal training. In 1910, he was elected to the New York State Senate, marking the beginning of his political career. His work in the Senate focused on progressive reform and improved working and living conditions.

In 1913, Franklin was appointed Assistant Secretary of the Navy by President Woodrow Wilson. During his time at the Navy Department, Roosevelt was committed to modernizing the American fleet and preparing for the coming global conflict.

In 1921, Roosevelt was diagnosed with poliomyelitis, a disease that left him paralyzed from the waist down. This personal challenge was a turning point in his life, but it did not discourage him. Despite physical limitations, Roosevelt continued his political career and focused on public service.

In 1928 he was elected Governor of New York. During his term, he implemented several progressive reforms that improved the economic and social conditions of the state, including the creation of an unemployment insurance system and the regulation of industries.

In 1932, Roosevelt was elected President of the United States in the context of the Great Depression. His campaign focused on the promise of a "New Deal" to confront the economic crisis.

The "New Deal" was a set of programs, reforms, and projects intended to alleviate the effects of the Great Depression, promote economic recovery, and reform the financial system. Roosevelt implemented several measures to address unemployment, industrial recovery, and financial reform.

Some of the most notable initiatives of the New Deal included:

The Unemployment Insurance Act: Established a federal unemployment insurance system and assisted workers who had lost their jobs.

The Social Security Act: Created a pension system for the elderly, widows, and orphans, and assisted people with disabilities.

The Works Projects Administration (WPA): Employed on infrastructure and public works projects, such as the construction of bridges, roads, and public buildings.

The Securities and Exchange Regulatory Act: Established the Securities and Exchange Commission (SEC) to regulate the securities market and prevent fraudulent financial practices.

The New Deal transformed the role of the federal government in American life and laid the groundwork for the modern welfare state. Roosevelt succeeded in restoring public confidence in the government and the financial system.

With the outbreak of World War II, Roosevelt took a stance of support for the Allies, despite America's initial neutrality. In 1941, President Roosevelt and British Prime Minister Winston Churchill met at the Atlantic Conference and issued the Atlantic Charter, which outlined postwar principles and the Allies' commitment to strive for victory.

Roosevelt played a crucial role in mobilizing American resources for the war. Through the Lend-Lease Act, the United States provided military and material assistance to Allied countries, such as the United Kingdom, the Soviet Union, and China.

Roosevelt's leadership during the war was decisive for Allied strategy, and his ability to coordinate with other world leaders, such as Churchill and Soviet leader Josef Stalin, was key to the success of the war efforts.

In 1944, Roosevelt was re-elected to a fourth presidential term, becoming the only president in U.S. history to serve more than two terms. During his final presidential term, Roosevelt faced growing concerns about the postwar era and the shaping of the new world order.

In April 1945, while at a rest home in Warm Springs, Georgia, Roosevelt suffered a stroke and passed away on April 12, 1945. His death marked the end of an era in American and world politics.

Franklin D. Roosevelt's legacy is profound and lasting. His ability to lead during the Great Depression and World War II left an indelible mark on American history. His implementation of the New Deal set precedents for the federal government's role in economics and social welfare, and his wartime leadership contributed significantly to the defeat of the Axis Powers and the establishment of the postwar world order.

Franklin D. Roosevelt was a monumental figure in 20th-century history. His ability to meet and overcome both economic and war challenges, along with his innovative economic and social policies, changed the course of American and global history. His legacy continues to influence politics and governance, and his ability to lead in times of crisis remains an example of the importance of leadership and resilience.

5. Adolf Hitler

Adolf Hitler was born in Braunau am Inn, a small town on the border between Austria and Germany, on April 20, 1889. He was the fourth of six children of Alois Hitler, a customs official, and Klara Hitler. His childhood was marked by several hardships, including the death of several of his siblings in infancy and a contentious relationship with his father, who was authoritarian and strict.

Hitler moved to Linz to attend high school but dropped out at age 16. His dream of becoming an artist took him to Vienna in 1907, where he attempted to enter the Academy of Fine Arts, but was rejected twice. During his time in Vienna, Hitler lived in poverty and developed a growing obsession with nationalist and anti-Semitic ideas that would influence his future ideology.

In 1913, Hitler moved to Munich, Germany, and enlisted in the Bavarian army at the outbreak of World War I. He fought in the war and was awarded the Iron Cross for bravery. The experience of war had a profound impact on him, reinforcing his sense of extreme nationalism and resentment toward the German defeat.

After the end of World War I, Hitler stayed in Munich and joined the National Socialist German Workers' Party (NSDAP) in 1920. Postwar Germany was marked by political and economic instability, and the NSDAP offered a nationalist and anti-Semitic platform that appealed to Hitler.

Hitler quickly rose within the NSDAP, and in 1921 became its leader. In 1923, he attempted a failed coup known as the "Beer Hall Putsch," which led to his imprisonment. During his time in prison, he wrote "Mein Kampf" ("My Struggle"), a book that laid out his vision of German nationalism, anti-Semitic racism, and the need for territorial expansion.

Following his release, Hitler used political and propaganda strategies to gain popular support. He took advantage of the economic crisis of the Great Depression to attract a broad base of support, promising to restore Germany's greatness and defy the Treaty of Versailles. His inflammatory rhetoric and ability to mobilize the masses led to significant growth in elections.

In January 1933, Hitler was appointed Chancellor of Germany. He quickly consolidated his power through a series of political moves and laws, such as the Act of Full Powers, which gave him dictatorial authority. In 1934, after the death of President Paul von Hindenburg, Hitler declared himself Führer, combining the roles of Chancellor and President.

Once in power, Hitler implemented a series of policies that transformed Germany into a totalitarian state based on Nazi ideology. This included:

Repression and Terror: The Gestapo (secret state police) and SS (Schutzstaffel) carried out a systematic campaign of repression against political opponents, Jews, and other groups deemed "undesirable." The Night of the Long Knives in 1934 eliminated many of his rivals within the party.

Anti-Semitism and the Holocaust: Hitler promoted an anti-Semitic agenda that culminated in the Holocaust, the systematic genocide of six million Jews and millions of other minority groups. Concentration and extermination camps were an integral part of this plan.

Expansionism and War: Hitler implemented a policy of territorial expansion, beginning with the annexation of Austria in 1938 and the occupation of Czechoslovakia. In 1939, the invasion of Poland triggered World War II. During the conflict, Germany aggressively expanded into Europe, leading to a global war that resulted in devastation on an unprecedented scale.

World War II proved to be a catastrophic conflict that ultimately led to Germany's defeat. As Allied forces advanced into German territory, Hitler's situation became increasingly desperate. In April 1945, with Berlin in ruins and Soviet forces at the gates of his bunker, Hitler committed suicide on April 30, 1945.

Hitler's influence on history is deeply negative, marked by the genocide of the Holocaust, the widespread destruction during World War II, and the legacy of Nazi ideology. His regime led to the creation of a totalitarian state that, being based on principles of racial hatred and extreme nationalism, caused global devastation and left an indelible mark on modern history.

Adolf Hitler is one of the most infamous figures in modern history, although adored by radical and violent groups. His influence in the 20th century was extremely destructive. His ability to manipulate social and political discontent and his radical vision led to the establishment of a totalitarian regime that unleashed a world war and systematic genocide. The impact of his actions remains a grim reminder of the dangers of extremism and intolerance. His legacy continues to be studied and analyzed to understand and prevent the recurrence of such destructive ideologies.

6. Joseph Stalin

Joseph Stalin (1878-1953), born Joseph Vissarionovich Dzhugashvili, was one of the most influential and controversial leaders of the 20th century. His rule of the Soviet Union from the mid-1920s until his death in 1953 was marked by profound political, social, and economic transformations, as well as brutal repression that left an indelible mark on human history.

Stalin was born in Gori, Georgia, then part of the Russian Empire, to a humble family. As a young man, he showed revolutionary inclinations and joined the Bolshevik movement, led by Vladimir Lenin. He was an effective organizer, using clandestine methods to promote the revolutionary cause. Stalin also acquired a reputation as a ruthless operator, carrying out bank robberies and other illegal acts to finance party activities.

Following the October Revolution of 1917, which brought the Bolsheviks to power, Stalin played several key roles in the new Soviet government. His political skill and loyalty to Lenin won him the trust of the

Bolshevik leader, who appointed him People's Commissar for Nationalities, a crucial position in managing the diverse ethnicities of the vast Soviet empire.

Upon Lenin's death in 1924, Stalin, who was then General Secretary of the Communist Party, began his definitive rise to power. Skillfully using his control over the party's bureaucratic apparatus, he managed to sideline his most notable rivals, such as Leon Trotsky, Grigori Zinoviev and Lev Kamenev, establishing himself as the supreme leader of the Soviet Union by the late 1920s.

Stalin's rule was characterized by absolute control over the state, the party and society. One of his first and most significant acts was the implementation of the Five-Year Plans, a series of economic programs designed to rapidly industrialize the country and increase agricultural production through the forced collectivization of land. Industrialization transformed the Soviet Union into a global power, but collectivization had devastating consequences, especially in Ukraine, where Stalinist policies contributed to the catastrophe of the Holodomor, a famine that caused millions of deaths between 1932 and 1933.

As Stalin consolidated his control, he also increased political repression. During the Great Purge of 1936-1938, thousands of army officers, party members, and ordinary citizens were arrested, executed, or sent to labor camps in the Gulag on charges of treason or counterrevolutionary activities. The purge was a tactic to eliminate any potential rivals and entrench his personal power, creating a state of terror that paralyzed the population.

During World War II, Stalin was instrumental in the Soviet resistance to the Nazi invasion in 1941, an operation that brought the USSR to the brink of defeat. Stalin initially made serious mistakes by ignoring warnings of an impending German attack, but quickly reorganized, assuming direct control of military strategy. Under his command, the Red Army defended Moscow, won the crucial Battle of Stalingrad in 1943, and eventually advanced to Berlin in 1945, contributing significantly to the defeat of Nazi Germany.

Despite his initial failings, Stalin's leadership during the war was crucial to the Soviet war effort, and the USSR emerged from the war as one of the world's two superpowers. The victory allowed Stalin to further consolidate his control over Eastern Europe, establishing communist regimes in countries such as Poland, Hungary, Romania, and East Germany, which would be the prelude to the Cold War.

Stalin died on March 5, 1953, but his legacy remains the subject of intense debate. In terms of economic impact, he transformed the Soviet Union into a major industrial and military power. Under his leadership, the USSR managed to develop nuclear weapons and expand its global influence, being one of the key pieces in the bipolar system that defined the geopolitics of the second half of the 20th century.

However, the human cost of his rule was staggering. Millions are estimated to have died because of famine, political repression, purges, and inhumane conditions in the Gulag camps. Stalin created a totalitarian system where dissent was crushed, and fear permeated all levels of society.

After his death, his successor, Nikita Khrushchev, condemned many of the excesses of Stalinism during the famous Secret Speech of 1956, marking the beginning of a policy of "de-Stalinization" that sought to eliminate the cult of personality that Stalin had fostered around him. Nevertheless, Stalin's influence on Soviet political culture endured, and his figure has been rehabilitated at times, especially in post-Soviet Russia, where some sectors revere him as a symbol of power and stability.

Stalin left a deeply ambivalent legacy: on the one hand, a visionary leader who managed to industrialize and modernize his country, and on the other, a tyrant whose policies led to the death and suffering of millions. The debate over his influence and legacy remains a central theme in modern historiography and in discussions about the nature of power and political repression.

7. Mao Zedong

Mao Zedong (1893-1976), also known as Mao Tse-Tung, was the Chinese revolutionary leader who founded the People's Republic of China in 1949. His rule marked an era of radical political, economic and social transformations, but also of brutal repression and humanitarian disasters. Under his leadership, China established itself as a global power, although its domestic policies, such as the Great Leap Forward and the Cultural Revolution, brought suffering to millions of people. Mao's legacy is deeply ambivalent, seen as both a visionary who changed the face of China and a dictator whose decisions led to enormous tragedies.

Mao Zedong was born into a relatively well-off peasant family in Hunan Province in southern China. From a young age, he was an avid reader and became interested in Marxism-Leninism following the October Revolution in Russia. In the 1920s, Mao joined the Chinese Communist Party (CCP) and quickly rose through its ranks, although his ideas about revolution diverged from the communist orthodoxy of the time.

Unlike communist leaders who saw the urban proletariat as the basis for a socialist revolution, Mao believed that the Chinese peasantry, who made up most of the population, was the true revolutionary engine. This stance distinguished him within the international communist movement and shaped his strategy in the years to come.

In the 1930s, the Chinese Communist Party waged a civil war against the Kuomintang (KMT), the ruling nationalist party led by Chiang Kai-shek. During this period, Mao emerged as the undisputed leader of the CCP. The key moment in his rise was the Long March (1934–35), a massive retreat of communist forces that crossed more than 9,000 kilometers to escape KMT encirclement. Although it was a tactical retreat, the

Long March cemented Mao as the party's supreme leader, and his figure became a symbol of resistance.

With the outbreak of World War II and the Japanese invasion of China, the CCP and KMT formed a temporary alliance to confront the common enemy. However, civil war between the two sides resumed after Japan's defeat in 1945. Finally, in 1949, communist forces defeated the Kuomintang, and Mao proclaimed the establishment of the People's Republic of China on October 1 of that year.

Upon coming to power, Mao Zedong began to consolidate his control over the new communist state. He implemented policies that transformed the country's agrarian structure, redistributing land from landlords to peasants, and then pushed for collectivization of agriculture, modeled on the Soviet model.

One of the key moments in his rule was the implementation of the Great Leap Forward (1958-1962), a campaign to accelerate industrialization and collectivization. Mao believed that China could overtake the Western powers in a short period through mass mobilization of the people. However, the Great Leap Forward was an economic disaster. Pressure to meet production quotas led to falsified reports and disorganization of agricultural production. As a result, between 15 and 45 million people died of starvation during a devastating famine, constituting one of the greatest human tragedies of the 20th century.

Following the failure of the Great Leap Forward, Mao's influence in government waned, but he returned to the scene in force in the mid-1960s with the launch of the Cultural Revolution (1966-1976). This campaign was an attempt by Mao to purge the Communist Party of elements he considered "counter-revolutionary" and reassert his absolute control. Millions of young people were mobilized into the Red Guards, who attacked party officials, intellectuals, and ordinary citizens, destroying symbols of traditional Chinese culture and carrying out a violent political purge.

The Cultural Revolution plunged China into chaos. The economy came to a standstill, educational institutions were closed, and millions of people were persecuted, imprisoned, or killed. Although Mao consolidated his power through this campaign, the social and cultural cost was incalculable.

As for foreign policy, Mao was a skilled strategist. Although he initially aligned China with the Soviet Union, ideological and geopolitical tensions between the two countries grew, resulting in a complete break in the 1960s, known as the Sino-Soviet split. Mao began to distance himself from the Soviet model and promoted his own version of communism, based on the peasantry and protracted armed struggle.

One of the most significant moments in Mao's foreign policy was the rapprochement with the United States in the early 1970s, culminating in US President Richard Nixon's historic visit to China in 1972. This strategic move not only allowed China to gain legitimacy on the international stage, but also played a key role in reconfiguring international relations during the Cold War.

Mao Zedong died on September 9, 1976, leaving behind a deeply contradictory legacy. On the one hand, he is revered for having transformed China into a unified and sovereign country, freed from imperialism and foreign intervention. Under his leadership, China emerged as a power with global influence, and the Chinese Communist Party consolidated a firm grip on the country's political life.

The costs of his rule, however, were enormous. Mao's policies, especially the Great Leap Forward and the Cultural Revolution, resulted in the deaths of tens of millions of people and the devastation of China's social and cultural structures. The Cultural Revolution, in particular, left deep scars on the nation's psyche, and its impact on education, culture, and human relations still resonates in contemporary China.

Following his death, his successor, Deng Xiaoping, pushed through a series of reforms that opened China's economy to the world and marked a move away from many Maoist policies, although the Communist Party has maintained the figure of Mao as a revolutionary icon. Mao's legacy remains a subject of debate inside and outside China, where some consider him the "founding father" of modern China, while others see him as an authoritarian leader whose policies brought devastation.

8. Martin Luther King Jr.

Martin Luther King Jr. (1929-1968) was one of the most influential leaders of the American civil rights movement and a global symbol of peaceful resistance against racial oppression. His vision of an America where people were judged by the "content of their character" and not the color of their skin made him an immortal figure in the fight for equality. Through his leadership in nonviolent protests and his role as an orator, King inspired millions to fight against racial segregation, discrimination, and social injustice. His legacy is inseparable from the history of civil rights and continues to shape discussions about social justice and racial equity today.

Martin Luther King Jr. was born on January 15, 1929, in Atlanta, Georgia, to a deeply religious, middle-class African American family. His father, Martin Luther King Sr., was an influential Baptist pastor, shaping King's path in the church and his moral approach to social justice. From a young age, King displayed exceptional intelligence and a keen capacity for leadership, graduating with honors in Sociology from Morehouse College at age 19.

King then attended Crozer Theological Seminary in Pennsylvania, where he became interested in Mahatma Gandhi's teachings on nonviolence as a tool for social justice. He also earned a doctorate in systematic theology from Boston University in 1955. During his studies, King developed a philosophical and theological vision based on Christian love and nonviolent resistance, which he would later apply in his fight for civil rights.

King's role as a leader of the civil rights movement began in 1955 with the Montgomery Bus Boycott, an event that changed the trajectory of the fight for racial equality in the United States. The protest was sparked by the arrest of Rosa Parks, an African American seamstress who refused to give up her seat on a bus to a white man, as required by segregation laws in the South.

King, then pastor of the Dexter Avenue Baptist Church in Montgomery, Alabama, was elected president of the newly formed Montgomery Improvement Association, which organized the boycott. Under his leadership, African Americans in Montgomery refused to ride the buses for more than a year, financially weakening the segregated public transportation system.

The boycott ended with a U.S. Supreme Court ruling declaring segregation on public buses unconstitutional, a significant triumph for the movement. This success cemented King as the foremost civil rights leader and convinced him that nonviolent civil disobedience was a powerful tool to combat racial injustice.

Throughout the 1960s, Martin Luther King Jr. led numerous protests and demonstrations that shook the foundations of racial segregation in the United States. In 1957, he co-founded the Southern Christian Leadership Conference (SCLC), an organization that sought to coordinate civil rights activism through nonviolence and the mobilization of African American churches. Under King's leadership, the SCLC played a crucial role in some of the most important protests of the time.

King understood that nonviolence did not mean passivity, but rather active and powerful resistance. Inspired by the teachings of Gandhi and his own Christian faith, King promoted peaceful civil disobedience, challenging unjust laws and exposing the brutality of racism. His tactics included sit-ins, marches, and boycotts, often facing brutal repression by local authorities and resistance from much of white society.

One of the most significant examples of this strategy was the Birmingham Campaign in 1963. King and other SCLC leaders organized demonstrations to desegregate public facilities in Birmingham, Alabama, one of the most segregated cities in the country. The violent response by Public Safety Commissioner Bull Connor, who used police dogs and water cannons against protesters, including children, was captured by the media and broadcast nationally, generating a wave of outrage and support for the civil rights movement.

One of the highlights of King's career was the March on Washington for Jobs and Freedom, held on August 28, 1963. More than 250,000 people gathered on the National Mall in Washington, D.C., to demand the elimination of segregationist laws and the creation of equal economic opportunities for African Americans.

At this event, King delivered his famous "I Have a Dream" speech, in which he expressed his vision of an America where all people were treated with equality and dignity. In his speech, King spoke of a future where "my four little children will live in a nation where they will not be judged by the color of their skin, but by the content of their character." This speech became an anthem of the struggle for civil rights and remains one of the most iconic in American history.

The march and the impact of King's speech played a key role in the passage of the Civil Rights Act of 1964, which banned segregation in public places and discrimination in employment. This was a landmark achievement for the movement, and King was awarded the Nobel Peace Prize in 1964 in recognition of his nonviolent leadership.

Despite the progress made with the Civil Rights Act, voting rights remained a challenge for African Americans, especially in the American South, where states-imposed barriers such as literacy tests and poll taxes to prevent blacks from voting. King turned his attention to this injustice, organizing the 1965 Selma to Montgomery marches to demand voting rights.

During one of the first marches, known as Bloody Sunday, police violently attacked unarmed protesters as they crossed the Edmund Pettus Bridge in Selma, Alabama. Images of police brutality shocked the country and put pressure on the federal government to act. Soon after, President Lyndon B. Johnson signed into law the Voting Rights Act of 1965, which banned discriminatory practices that prevented African Americans from voting, marking another historic victory for the movement led by King.

In the later years of his life, King began to expand his activism to address issues of poverty, economic inequality, and the Vietnam War. In 1967, he gave a speech titled "Beyond Vietnam," where he openly criticized the war and U.S. military intervention, earning him criticism from many, including allies within the civil rights movement.

Despite rising tensions and discontent among certain sectors of society, King continued to lead the movement until his assassination on April 4, 1968, in Memphis, Tennessee, where he was supporting a sanitation workers' strike. He was assassinated by a sniper, James Earl Ray, at the age of 39, shocking the nation and the entire world.

Martin Luther King Jr.'s legacy is monumental. His commitment to nonviolence and social justice transformed not only the United States but also the global human rights movement. Through his leadership, landmark laws such as the Civil Rights Act of 1964 and the Voting Rights Act of 1965 were passed, breaking down institutionalized barriers of racism and segregation.

King not only challenged the racist system of his time but also showed the power of moral activism and peaceful resistance. His message of equality, love, and justice remains a source of inspiration for struggles against discrimination and oppression around the world. Every year on the third Monday in January, the United States celebrates Martin Luther King Jr. Day, a holiday honoring his life and legacy.

His influence transcends borders, and his teachings on nonviolence, justice, and equality continue to shape contemporary struggles for human rights and social justice.

9. John F. Kennedy

John Fitzgerald Kennedy (1917-1963), commonly known as JFK, was the 35th president of the United States, serving from 1961 until his assassination in 1963. His brief tenure was marked by pivotal moments in world history, including the Cuban Missile Crisis, the start of the Space Race, and the American Civil Rights Movement. Although his presidency was tragically cut short, his charisma, progressive vision, and ability to lead in times of tension made him a political icon. Over the years, Kennedy has been remembered as a representation of postwar idealism, and his legacy continues to influence American and global politics.

John F. Kennedy was born on May 29, 1917, in Brookline, Massachusetts, to a wealthy and politically active family. He was the second son of Joseph P. Kennedy, an influential businessman and diplomat, and Rose Fitzgerald, whose father had been mayor of Boston. The Kennedys were a prominent family in politics and the business world, allowing John and his siblings to grow up in an environment of power and expectations of public success.

Kennedy attended Harvard University, where he excelled as a student and developed his interest in international politics. In 1940, he wrote his senior thesis on British policy toward Nazism, which was later published as the book "Why England Slept." This work was an early sign of his flair for geopolitical analysis.

During World War II, Kennedy served as an officer in the United States Navy in the Pacific, where he commanded a torpedo patrol boat (PT-109). His bravery during a mission in which his ship was sunk and his leadership in saving his crew earned him recognition and medals, fueling the heroic legend that would surround his political career.

After the war, Kennedy began his political career with the support of his influential family. In 1946, he was elected to the House of Representatives from the state of Massachusetts. During his time in Congress, he developed a reputation as a pragmatic and progressive politician. In 1952, he was elected to the United States Senate, defeating Republican incumbent Henry Cabot Lodge Jr. in a close campaign.

During his time in the Senate, Kennedy championed positions that balanced a progressive approach to social issues with a strong stance on foreign policy, especially about the Cold War. He also struggled with health problems, suffering from chronic illnesses, including Addison's disease, which he hid from the public. Despite his health challenges, Kennedy was emerging as one of the most promising figures in American politics.

In 1960, Kennedy decided to run for president, and in a fiercely contested campaign, he faced Vice President Richard Nixon. The 1960 election was historic in many ways, including the first series of televised presidential debates, where Kennedy's charismatic and youthful image contrasted with Nixon's seriousness. Kennedy won the election by a narrow margin, becoming the youngest president ever elected and the first Catholic to hold the office.

John F. Kennedy assumed the presidency at one of the tensest moments in global history, amid the Cold War when the United States and the Soviet Union were competing for military, political, and technological dominance. His administration was characterized by a combination of boldness, charisma, and a pragmatic approach to meeting these challenges.

One of his first tests of fire was the Bay of Pigs invasion in 1961, a failed attempt to overthrow Fidel Castro's government in Cuba by CIA-backed Cuban exiles. The failure of the invasion was a severe blow to Kennedy's credibility, but he learned from the experience, and this prepared him for his handling of the Cuban Missile Crisis in 1962, one of the most critical moments of his presidency.

The Missile Crisis was triggered when it was discovered that the Soviet Union was installing nuclear missiles in Cuba, just 90 miles from American shores. For 13 days in October 1962, the world was on the brink of nuclear war. However, Kennedy, through a combination of firmness and diplomacy, negotiated with Soviet leader Nikita Khrushchev to remove the missiles in exchange for a public promise that the United States would not invade Cuba and a secret agreement to remove American missiles in Turkey. His handling of this crisis was widely praised and cemented his reputation as a firm leader capable of handling situations of extreme pressure.

On the domestic front, Kennedy pushed through a series of reforms under what he called the "New Frontier" program. Although his agenda faced obstacles in Congress, where many of his projects were blocked, he promoted initiatives in education, health care, and social welfare. He also advocated for greater investment in science and technology, marking the beginning of the space race. In a historic speech in 1962, Kennedy announced the ambitious goal of landing a man on the Moon before the end of the decade. This commitment boosted NASA's space program, which would culminate in the successful Apollo 11 moon landing in 1969.

One of the most important aspects of Kennedy's legacy was his growing support for the civil rights movement. While he was cautious early in his term so as not to alienate Southern Democrats who supported racial segregation, increasing unrest and racial violence across the country pushed him to take a more decisive stance.

In 1963, following violent incidents in Birmingham, Alabama, where security forces brutally attacked peaceful protesters, Kennedy spoke out strongly in favor of racial equality. In a televised address, he expressed his support for the cause of civil rights, stating that "this nation, for all its inhabitants, will not be completely free until all its citizens are free." Kennedy introduced a bill to Congress to end segregation in public places and guarantee voting rights for African Americans.

Although the Civil Rights Act was not passed during his term, his support paved the way for the Civil Rights Act of 1964, which was enacted after his assassination under his successor, Lyndon B. Johnson. His relationship with leaders of the movement, such as

Martin Luther King Jr., was also key to legitimizing the federal approach to the fight for racial equality.

On November 22, 1963, during a visit to Dallas, Texas, John F. Kennedy was assassinated while traveling in an open-top car. Lee Harvey Oswald was arrested as the prime suspect in the crime, but his assassination two days later left many unanswered questions and fueled conspiracy theories that persist to this day.

Kennedy's assassination was a devastating blow to America and the world, and his death marked the abrupt end of an era of hope and change. His funeral was a globally televised event that symbolized the collective mourning of the loss of a charismatic leader who had inspired millions with his vision of a better world.

Kennedy also left a legacy through his inspiring vision of public service. His call for citizens to "ask, not, what their country can do for them, but what they can do for their country" continues to resonate with subsequent generations. Furthermore, his commitment to diplomacy and global peace remains a benchmark for world leaders.

His presidency, though brief, was seen as a promise of what America could be: a more just, technologically advanced, and peaceful country. The John F. Kennedy Foundation and the JFK Presidential Library continue to preserve his legacy, and his name remains synonymous with hope, visionary leadership, and public service.

10. Pablo Picasso

Pablo Picasso (1881-1973) was a revolutionary painter, sculptor, and creator who transformed the art world in the 20th century. As one of the founders of Cubism and a key figure in the evolution of modern art, his influence was immense, not only for his ability to break with conventions but also for the profound diversity of his work, which spanned multiple styles and techniques. Throughout his life, Picasso produced more than 50,000 works, ranging from painting and sculpture to ceramics and printmaking. His contributions to art remain fundamental to the history of creativity, and his legacy has left an indelible mark on generations of artists.

Pablo Picasso was born Pablo Diego José Francisco de Paula Juan Nepomuceno Crispín Crispiniano María Remedios de la Santísima Trinidad Ruiz Picasso was born on October 25, 1881, in Málaga, Spain, to a middle-class family. His father, José Ruiz Blasco, was an art teacher and painter, which allowed Picasso to be immersed in the artistic world from a very early age. As a child, he demonstrated an early talent for drawing and painting, even surpassing his father in skill at an early age.

Picasso studied at art academies in Barcelona and Madrid, although he was not a traditional student. He always showed a rebellion towards academic norms and artistic conventions of the time. During his teenage years, Picasso spent time in Paris, which was then the epicenter of European art. This move was decisive for his career, as it connected him with avant-garde movements and exposed him to a wide range of influences, such as Impressionism, Symbolism, and African art.

At the beginning of the 20th century, Picasso lived through what is known as his "blue period" (1901-1904), a period in which his work was dominated by cold tones and melancholic themes. This phase was influenced by the death of his close friend, Carlos Casagemas, which plunged him into deep sadness. Works from this stage, such as "The Old Guitarist" and "Life", depict marginalized, poor, and lonely figures, reflecting his pessimistic view of the world at the time.

Towards 1905, Picasso's work took a more optimistic and luminous turn, entering his "rose period." In this period, he began to use warmer colors, and his themes became more cheerful, depicting circus performers, harlequins, and bohemian characters. Works such as "Family of Saltimbanquis" are emblematic of this time. This phase marked an important transition towards his exploration of new artistic forms and techniques.

Beginning in 1907, Picasso embarked on what would become one of the most revolutionary achievements in the history of art: Cubism. Together with Georges Braque, Picasso developed a new artistic approach that broke with the tradition of linear perspective, introducing a fragmented representation of reality through geometric shapes. Cubism sought to show the multiple points of view of an object or figure on a single plane, which led to a more abstract and conceptual representation of the world.

One of the most emblematic works of this phase is "Les Demoiselles d'Avignon" (1907), a painting showing five female figures with distorted bodies and faces influenced by African masks. This work is considered the beginning of Cubism and caused great controversy in its time due to its radical rejection of the conventional human form.

Cubism evolved in two phases: Analytical Cubism (characterized by the fragmentation of the figure and the monochromatic color palette) and Synthetic Cubism (where Picasso and Braque began to reintroduce brighter colors and use collage as a technique). Cubism not only influenced painting, but also sculpture and other art forms, and transformed the course of modern art.

Picasso's life and work were deeply affected by the political events of his time, particularly the Spanish Civil War (1936-1939). Although he lived in Paris, Picasso closely followed the conflict in his native country and openly opposed the fascist regime of Francisco Franco.

His most iconic work about this conflict is "Guernica" (1937), a monumental mural commissioned by the Spanish Republican government for the Paris International Exposition. "Guernica" depicts the bombing of the Basque city of the same name by Nazi and fascist planes, an attack that caused the deaths of hundreds of civilians. This work, in shades of white, black, and grey, is a powerful denunciation of the horrors of war and has become a universal symbol of the fight against oppression and violence. With its chaotic composition, twisted figures, and animals in agony, "Guernica" remains one of the most influential and talked about works of the 20th century.

Picasso's power lay not only in his ability to create new art forms but also in his ability to influence other artists and movements. His ability to constantly reinvent himself, exploring different styles and techniques, from Cubism to Surrealism, kept him at the forefront of art for more than six decades. Picasso was a pioneer in the integration of mixed media into his work, using techniques such as collage, assemblage, and printmaking, making him a precursor of contemporary art.

In addition to his innovative artistic work, Picasso was a central figure in the European and global art community. His studio at the Bateau-Lavoir in Paris was a meeting point for many of the most influential artists and intellectuals of his time, such as Henri Matisse, Guillaume Apollinaire, and Amedeo Modigliani. Picasso exerted considerable influence on his contemporaries and later generations, who saw him as a leader and a reference in the continuous exploration of new forms of expression.

Throughout his career, Picasso proved versatile not only in painting but also in sculpture, ceramics, poetry, and even in the creation of costumes and sets for ballet. His ability to master multiple disciplines established him as one of the most complete and influential artists in history.

Picasso's personal life was as complex and multifaceted as his work. He was involved in romantic relationships with several women throughout his life, many of whom were important muses and inspirations for his art. Among them, Fernande Olivier, Olga Khokhlova, Dora Maar, Françoise Gilot, and

Jacqueline Roque stand out. Each of these women marked different phases in his artistic life, and their portraits are present in many of his works.

While Picasso was admired for his artistic genius, his private life was marked by controversy. He was known for his conflictual and sometimes abusive relationships with the women in his life, which has generated debates around his figure in contemporary times.

Pablo Picasso died on April 8, 1973, at the age of 91, leaving an unrivaled legacy in the art world. His ability to challenge norms, continually reinvent himself, and push the boundaries of creativity made him a giant in art history. Through Cubism, Surrealism, and many other stylistic explorations, Picasso not only influenced his contemporaries but broke new ground for modern and contemporary art.

Picasso's works can be found in the most important museums in the world, and his impact lives on art today. Picasso is seen as the archetype of the modern artist, a creator who, with his inexhaustible energy and insatiable desire for innovation, forever transformed the way we understand art.

11. Steve Jobs

Steve Jobs (1955-2011) was an entrepreneur, inventor, and pioneer in the world of technology, best known for being the co-founder of Apple Inc. and for leading the creation of iconic products such as the iPhone, iPad, and Macintosh. Jobs transformed not only the technology industry but also the way people interact with technology, entertainment, and communication. With a mix of creativity, innovation, and a deep sense of design, Jobs left a legacy that continues to influence multiple industries. His ability to lead teams toward the creation of products that would change the world made him one of the most important figures of the 21st century.

Steve Paul Jobs was born on February 24, 1955, in San Francisco, California, and was adopted by Paul and Clara Jobs. From a young age, Jobs showed a keen curiosity about technology and electronics, influenced by his father, who taught him how to work with tools and repair electronic items in their garage. Although a brilliant student, Jobs had a rebellious personality, which led to him being a troublemaker in his youth.

In 1972, Jobs enrolled at Reed College in Oregon, but dropped out of formal studies after only one semester. Despite dropping out of college, he continued to attend classes informally, taking a particular interest in calligraphy courses, something that later influenced the design of typefaces on early Macintosh computers.

After leaving Reed College, Jobs traveled to India in search of spiritual inspiration, where he experimented with Buddhism and Eastern mysticism. These experiences would profoundly influence his minimalist approach and his thinking about design and simplicity in the technology products he would later develop.

In 1976, along with his friend Steve Wozniak and entrepreneur Ronald Wayne, Jobs co-founded Apple Computer in the garage of his home in Los Altos, California. Jobs' vision was clear: he wanted to make computers accessible and easy to use for the public, not just tech-savvy people. Up until that point, computers were bulky, complicated, and out of reach for the average user.

Apple's first product, the Apple I, was a computer designed by Wozniak and sold as a kit. However, it was with the Apple II (1977) that the company began to gain traction. The Apple II was one of the first commercially successful personal computers, turning Apple into a growth company.

In 1984, Apple launched the Macintosh, a revolutionary personal computer that featured a graphical user interface and a mouse, something that was groundbreaking at the time. The famous Super Bowl ad directed by Ridley Scott, which compared the launch of the Macintosh to George Orwell's novel "1984," marked a milestone in marketing history. Although the Macintosh's initial success was modest, this machine laid the groundwork for what would become Apple's approach: seamless integration of hardware and software, with a user-centered design.

Despite the success of the Macintosh, Jobs was known for his intense leadership style and volatile temper. In 1985, following an internal power struggle, he was ousted from Apple, a company he had co-founded. This dismissal was a devastating blow to Jobs, but in retrospect, he would describe it as one of the best things that ever happened to him.

After he departed from Apple, Jobs founded NeXT, a high-end business and education-oriented computing company. Although NeXT's products were not a huge commercial success, the company produced significant technological advances that would later influence the development of Apple. NeXT's operating system would serve as the basis for macOS when Jobs returned to Apple years later.

In parallel, in 1986 Jobs acquired The Graphics Group, a small computer graphics division of Lucasfilm that would later become Pixar Animation Studios. Under Jobs' direction, Pixar produced the first fully computer-animated feature film, "Toy Story" (1995), which was a massive critical and commercial success. Pixar not only revolutionized digital animation but also redefined animated filmmaking in general. Eventually, Jobs sold Pixar to Disney in 2006, making him Disney's largest individual shareholder.

In 1997, Apple, which was struggling financially, purchased NeXT for $429 million, allowing Jobs to return to the company he had co-founded. Upon returning to Apple, Jobs assumed the role of interim CEO, which became known as "iCEO." Within a short time, Jobs reorganized Apple's structure, eliminating unprofitable products and focusing on a clear vision: making technology products simple, elegant, and powerful.

In 1998, Apple launched the iMac, an all-in-one personal computer with a colorful, futuristic design. The iMac was a resounding success and marked Apple's rebirth as a leader in the technology industry. Under Jobs' leadership, Apple not only became profitable again but also became one of the most innovative and admired companies in the world.

In the years that followed, Jobs and his team would once again revolutionize the industry with a series of groundbreaking products that redefined consumer technology:

In 2001, the launch of the iPod changed the way people listened to music. The iPod, along with the iTunes music store, revolutionized the music industry by making digital song downloads accessible and easy to use.

In 2007, Jobs introduced the iPhone, a device that not only combined a mobile phone with a music player and camera but also introduced the idea of mobile apps. The iPhone not only transformed the mobile phone industry, but it also ushered in the smartphone era, which would radically change the way people communicate, work, and consume media.

In 2010, Jobs introduced the iPad, a tablet computer that popularized the concept of mobile devices larger than phones but more portable than laptops. The iPad quickly became a hit product in sectors such as education, business, and entertainment.

Under his leadership, Apple went from being on the verge of bankruptcy to becoming the most valuable company in the world, with a market capitalization that surpassed $1 trillion after his death.

Jobs' success was largely due to his unique leadership style. He was known for being extremely demanding, with high standards for both himself and others. He was not afraid to reject ideas that did not meet his vision and demanded perfection in product design and functionality. Although he was often described as a difficult person, he was also able to inspire those around him to exceptional levels of creativity and innovation.

One of Jobs' most distinctive traits was his obsession with design. It was not just about making functional products, but about creating devices that were beautiful and enjoyable to use. Jobs firmly believed that design was not just about how something looked, but how it worked. This philosophy is reflected in all of Apple's products, which are noted for both their simplicity and meticulous attention to detail.

Steve Jobs passed away on October 5, 2011, at the age of 56, after a long battle with pancreatic cancer. His death was met with an outpouring of tributes from around the world, from business leaders to entertainment and political figures. His impact on technology, design, and culture was immense, and his legacy lives on through Apple and the many innovations he helped create.

His visionary approach and ability to see beyond the technological limitations of his time continue to inspire entrepreneurs and innovators around the world. Apple, the company he founded and led, remains one of the most influential companies in the world and continues to produce innovations that define our era.

12. Bill Gates

Bill Gates (1955), co-founder of Microsoft, is one of the most influential businessmen of the modern era. His vision of software and his role in the personal computing revolution forever changed the way the world uses computers. As an engineer, businessman, and philanthropist, Gates has left an indelible mark on multiple spheres, from technology to health and global development. His legacy extends not only through Microsoft, but also through his foundation, the Bill & Melinda Gates Foundation, which has had a significant impact on reducing poverty, improving public health, and fighting global diseases.

William Henry Gates III was born on October 28, 1955, in Seattle, Washington, to an upper-class family. His father, William H. Gates Sr., was a prominent lawyer, and his mother, Mary Maxwell Gates, was an executive at nonprofit organizations and a trustee of the University of Washington. From a young age, Gates showed a notable interest in technology and mathematics. At the age of 13, at the exclusive Lakeside School, he had his first contact with a computer, and together with his friend Paul Allen, he began programming.

Gates proved to be a prodigy in the use of software. In 1973, he entered Harvard University, where he studied mathematics and computer science. However, Gates dropped out of Harvard in 1975 to devote himself entirely to his project with Allen: creating software for the first personal computers, a move that would define the future of computing and change his life forever.

In 1975, Gates and Paul Allen founded Microsoft (initially "Micro-Soft") to develop software for personal computers. Their first big break came when they signed a contract with MITS, a company that made a microcomputer called the Altair 8800, to provide a programming language called Altair BASIC. This was Microsoft's first commercial success and marked the beginning of the path to dominance of the software market.

In 1980, Microsoft secured a crucial contract with IBM, the computer giant at the time, to provide the operating system for its new personal computers. Microsoft acquired an operating system called QDOS, adapted it, and renamed it MS-DOS. This deal was one of the most important strategic moves in the history of technology. Although IBM initially dominated the hardware, Microsoft retained the rights to the software, allowing MS-DOS to become the standard for the personal computer industry.

The real change came in 1985 when Microsoft released the first version of Windows, an operating system with a graphical user interface. Although the first version of Windows was modest in popularity, over time, Microsoft dominated the operating system market. In 1990, the release of Windows 3.0 was a smashing success and cemented Microsoft as the leader in personal computer software.

Under Gates' leadership, Microsoft expanded rapidly, introducing a series of products that became standard in the business and home worlds, such as Microsoft Office, which integrated programs like Word, Excel, and PowerPoint. The combination of Windows and Office transformed computers into essential tools for productivity around the world, both in businesses and homes.

Gates stood out not only for his ability to identify market opportunities but also for his ability to make strategic decisions and control every aspect of the company. His vision of "a computer on every desk and in every home" was revolutionary at a time when computers were seen as specialized tools. Gates was also known for his aggressive and competitive approach to business, which led to Microsoft being a dominant force in the technology industry.

In the 1990s, Microsoft became the largest software company in the world, and Bill Gates, with a major stake in the company, became the richest man on the planet, a title he held for many years. As the company grew, it also faced criticism and legal challenges. In 1998, the U.S. government sued Microsoft for anticompetitive practices, arguing that the company had used its dominant position in the operating system market to stifle competition. Despite the legal battles, which culminated in a settlement in 2001, Microsoft's dominance in the software market was not significantly threatened.

In 2000, Gates surprised the world by stepping down as Microsoft's CEO, handing over leadership to Steve Ballmer, though he continued to be involved as chairman and chief software architect. This move marked a transition in Gates' life, as he began to increasingly focus his efforts on philanthropy through the Bill & Melinda Gates Foundation, an organization he and his wife Melinda founded in 2000.

The Gates Foundation quickly became one of the largest and most influential philanthropic organizations in the world, focused on improving health, reducing poverty, and increasing access to education and technology. Its most notable initiatives include fighting diseases such as HIV/AIDS, tuberculosis, malaria, and polio, and improving sanitation and access to water in the world's most impoverished regions.

One of Gates' most notable contributions to global health was his commitment to eradicating polio, a disease that has been virtually eliminated in much of the world thanks to vaccination efforts supported by the Gates Foundation.

Gates has also played a crucial role in the fight against malaria, investing in research to develop new vaccines and treatments.

Gates was also an advocate for Global Access to Medicines. He worked to ensure that vaccines and medical treatments were accessible at affordable prices in developing countries, using his foundation's influence to negotiate deals with pharmaceutical companies and governments.

Another of Gates' major interests has been education. The Gates Foundation has invested billions of dollars in educational reform, especially in the United States, promoting access to technology in classrooms and improving the quality of teaching. Gates strongly believes in the power of education to reduce poverty and has worked on initiatives to support teachers and vulnerable students.

Gates has also used his influence in the technological field to promote access to technology and connectivity around the world. His vision of "digital inclusion" has been key to bridging the digital divide in many countries, allowing underprivileged communities to access technological tools that can improve their quality of life.

In 2008, Gates left his full-time position at Microsoft to devote himself entirely to philanthropy, although he remained involved as chairman of the board until 2014 when he finally retired from an active role in the company.

Throughout his life, Gates has been a controversial figure, both admired and criticized for his competitive approach to business. However, his impact on modern technology is indisputable. His vision of personal computing transformed the software industry and laid the groundwork for the era of consumer technology.

Gates is also one of the most influential figures in global philanthropy. Through his foundation, he has committed billions of dollars to humanitarian, health and education projects, and has influenced the behavior of other billionaires through initiatives such as The Giving Pledge, in which Gates and other philanthropists commit to donating at least half of their wealth to charitable causes.

Gates has also been an advocate of climate change in recent years, investing in clean technologies and renewable energy to combat global warming. He has highlighted the need for technological innovation to address climate problems and has published books and given lectures on the subject.

His legacy extends beyond technology, to a deep commitment to improving the living conditions of millions of people around the world. His ability to combine an entrepreneurial vision with a sense of social duty makes him a reference not only in the business world but also in the humanitarian field.

13. Elon Musk

Elon Musk (1971) is one of the most influential and controversial entrepreneurs of the modern era, known for his ability to transform entire industries with his disruptive and innovative approach. As founder and CEO of companies such as SpaceX, Tesla, Neuralink, and The Boring Company, Musk has played a crucial role in revolutionizing space technology, electric vehicles, artificial intelligence, and urban infrastructure. His vision encompasses not only Earth but also space exploration, to make humanity a multi-planetary species. With a mix of genius, audacity, and ambition, Musk has left a deep mark on modern technology and challenged traditional industry conventions.

Elon Reeve Musk was born on June 28, 1971, in Pretoria, South Africa, to a wealthy family. His father, Errol Musk, was an engineer, and his mother, Maye Musk, was a dietician and model. From a young age, Musk showed an intense curiosity about science and technology. By age 10, he was already programming, and by age 12, he created and sold his first software, a video game called Blastar.

Musk had a difficult childhood, marked by bullying and a strained relationship with his father. At age 17, he decided to leave South Africa and move to Canada, where he gained citizenship through his mother. He briefly studied at Queen's University before transferring to the University of Pennsylvania in the United States, where he earned a bachelor's degree in physics and another in economics at the Wharton School of Business.

Musk was subsequently accepted into Stanford's PhD program in applied physics but dropped out after just two days to pursue his entrepreneurial dreams in the burgeoning world of the Internet.

Musk's first major venture was Zip2, a software company founded in 1996, which provided maps and business directories for online newspapers. With the help of his brother Kimbal, Elon developed Zip2 to make digital information easier to access. In 1999, Compaq acquired Zip2 for $307 million, giving Musk his first major financial success.

With the capital raised from the sale of Zip2, Musk founded X.com in 1999, an online payments company. This company eventually merged with Confinity, which had a money transfer service called PayPal. Musk, as the largest shareholder and visionary leader, played a key role in the growth of PayPal, which became a global online payments platform. In 2002, eBay acquired PayPal for $1.5 billion, cementing Musk's reputation as a successful entrepreneur and giving him the financial resources to embark on more ambitious projects.

The next big step in Musk's career was founding SpaceX (Space Exploration Technologies Corp.) in 2002 to reduce the costs of access to space and, in the long term, colonizing Mars. Musk was convinced that the future of humanity depended on its ability to expand beyond Earth. Despite initial criticism and obstacles, SpaceX has achieved several unprecedented milestones in the aerospace industry.

In 2008, after several failed launches that brought the company to the brink of collapse, SpaceX successfully launched the Falcon 1, becoming the first private company to put a liquid-fueled rocket into orbit. Since then, SpaceX has continued to revolutionize the space industry with key technological advances, such as the Falcon 9, a reusable rocket, and the Dragon spacecraft, which has transported cargo and astronauts to the International Space Station (ISS).

In 2020, SpaceX made history by being the first private company to take astronauts to the ISS, ushering in a new era in commercial space exploration. But Musk doesn't stop there; his long-term vision with SpaceX is to build the Starship, capable of taking humans to Mars, to make the red planet a second base for humanity.

In parallel with his work at SpaceX, Musk also transformed the automotive industry. Although he was not the founder of Tesla, he joined the company shortly after its creation in 2004 and became its largest investor and CEO. Tesla was founded to accelerate the world's transition to sustainable energy by producing electric vehicles. Musk saw the potential of electric cars not only as an eco-friendly alternative but as the future of mobility.

In 2008, Tesla launched its first car, the Roadster, a fully electric sports car that broke the perception that electric cars were slow and unattractive. Tesla subsequently introduced a series of vehicles that revolutionized the market: the Model S, a luxury sedan; the Model X, an SUV; and the Model 3, which was designed to be an affordable electric car for the mass market.

Tesla has pioneered the development of long-lasting batteries and autonomous driving technologies, positioning itself as a leader in the electric vehicle industry. Over the years, Tesla has faced multiple challenges, from production issues to widespread skepticism from the traditional automotive industry. However, under Musk's leadership, Tesla has defied all expectations, becoming the most valuable automotive company in the world and catapulting Musk to the position of the richest person on the planet in 2021.

In addition, Tesla has also played a key role in the transition to renewable energy through its energy division, Tesla Energy, which develops home batteries and large-scale energy storage solutions, such as the Powerwall and the Powerpack.

Elon Musk is not limited to SpaceX and Tesla. His interests span a variety of fields that aim to solve global problems and future technological challenges.

14. Vladimir Putin

Vladimir Putin, born on October 7, 1952, in Leningrad (now St. Petersburg), is one of the most influential and controversial leaders of the 21st century. Since coming to power in 1999, Putin has transformed Russia into a central player in global politics, consolidating an authoritarian regime and pursuing an aggressive foreign policy that has reconfigured the international balance of power. His exercise of power has been marked by the centralization of control, the repression of internal opposition, and the revitalization of Russian national pride, all of which define his legacy.

Putin was born into a humble family in the Soviet Union. His father was a combatant in World War II and his mother was a factory worker. From a young age, Putin showed an interest in martial arts and espionage, which led him to join the KGB, the Soviet Union's intelligence and security agency, in 1975. During his time in the KGB, Putin specialized in foreign espionage and was posted to Dresden, East Germany, between 1985 and 1990, where he was involved in intelligence activities during the twilight of the Cold War.

When the Soviet Union collapsed in 1991, Putin returned to Leningrad (now renamed St. Petersburg) and began his transition into civilian politics. His relationship with Anatoly Sobchak, the mayor of St. Petersburg, helped him enter local government, where he began to build a network of political contacts. In 1996, Putin moved to Moscow, where he joined the team of then-President Boris Yeltsin.

In 1999, Yeltsin, weakened by health problems and corruption scandals, named Putin as his successor by appointing him prime minister. In December of that year, Yeltsin unexpectedly resigned, and Putin took over as interim president. In the March 2000 elections, Putin was elected president of Russia by a clear victory.

Putin's first term was marked by his effort to restore stability to Russia after the chaotic post-Soviet period of the 1990s. He inherited a country weakened by economic crisis, separatism in Chechnya, and widespread corruption. To meet these challenges, Putin centralized power in the Kremlin and reformed the political system, weakening the influence of the oligarchs who had accumulated power during Yeltsin's presidency.

One of Putin's first major challenges was the second war in Chechnya (1999-2009), a breakaway region seeking independence from Russia. Putin took a tough stance, launching a military offensive that resulted in the devastation of the region and thousands of deaths, but which ultimately consolidated Kremlin control over Chechnya. The victory in Chechnya was presented by Putin as a restoration of order in Russia, which increased his popularity among Russians.

Throughout his first term, Putin also centralized control over Russia's regions, limiting the autonomy of regional governors and eliminating direct elections for those positions, allowing him to consolidate a system of vertical power in which the Kremlin had direct control over regional administrations.

In economic terms, Putin took advantage of the boom in oil prices to revitalize the Russian economy. His government implemented reforms that promoted macroeconomic stability and allowed the accumulation of large foreign exchange reserves. This helped reduce public debt and strengthen the ruble, which in turn contributed to the revival of Russian nationalism.

During this period, Putin promoted the idea of a strong and sovereign Russia, regaining some of the superpower status it had lost with the collapse of the Soviet Union. He strengthened state control over strategic sectors such as energy, nationalizing or taking stakes in major companies such as Gazprom and Rosneft. The Russian economy began to grow, and millions of Russians experienced improvements in their standard of living.

In 2008, at the end of his second term, Putin respected the constitutional limitation that prevented a third consecutive term. However, he remained in power as prime minister while his close ally, Dmitry Medvedev, assumed the presidency. Although Medvedev was officially president, it was clear that Putin remained the true leader of Russia.

During this period, the Medvedev-Putin tandem pursued a more open foreign policy, promoting some cooperation with the West, such as the agreement to reduce nuclear arsenals. However, internally, Putin's power remained unshaken.

In 2012, Putin returned to the presidency after an election that sparked large protests in Moscow and other cities. His return marked the end of the brief experiment in liberalization and was accompanied by a series of more repressive measures to silence the opposition and control the media.

One of the most significant moments of Putin's leadership on the global stage was the annexation of Crimea in 2014. Following the fall of the pro-Russian government in Ukraine and the outbreak of the crisis in the country, Russia invaded and annexed the Crimean Peninsula, which was widely condemned by the international community and led to sanctions by the United States and the European Union.

The conflict in Ukraine and the annexation of Crimea marked a turning point in relations between Russia and the West. Putin justified the action as a defense of ethnic Russians in Crimea and an effort to restore Russian influence in world decisions. This action was celebrated in Russia, where Putin was perceived as a defender of national interests in the face of a hostile West. However, economic sanctions began to weaken

Russia's economy, which is dependent on foreign trade and energy exports.

Despite the sanctions, Putin has continued to challenge the Western-led world order, using tools such as military intervention in Syria, support for authoritarian regimes, and disinformation campaigns and cyberattacks to destabilize Western democracies. Under his rule, Russia has intervened in the conflicts in Ukraine and Syria, consolidating its position as a key military and geopolitical power in these regions.

At home, Putin's regime has been characterized by strict control over the media and the repression of any significant political dissent. Russia's major media outlets are either under state control or controlled by businessmen loyal to Putin, which has allowed the Kremlin to control the political narrative. However, it is also true that the major Western media outlets are not always transparent and free of interest when it comes to analyzing the Russian leader's actions.

Repression of the opposition has been a central aspect of Putin's tenure. Over the years, several Kremlin critics have been silenced in different ways. Some have been jailed, such as opposition leader Alexei Navalny, who died in captivity, while others, such as journalist Anna Politkovskaya and politician Boris Nemtsov, were killed under suspicious circumstances. Navalny has been one of the most prominent voices against corruption in Russia, and his poisoning in 2020, followed by his arrest, sparked international condemnation.

Putin's legacy is complex and polarizing. For many Russians, Putin is seen as the leader who restored Russia's stability, pride, and global influence after the chaos of the post-Soviet era. His administration has bolstered the economy, strengthened Russia's military capability, and rekindled a sense of national greatness.

However, his tenure has also been marked by the concentration of power, the repression of civil liberties, and the deterioration of relations with the West. The lack of a genuine democratic system, with elections not seen as fair by many observers, and persistent corruption have left Russia in a position of economic dependence on oil and gas.

Internationally, Putin has repositioned Russia as a challenging power to the West, using both military and cyber tactics to influence global affairs. His legacy will be deeply linked to his authoritarian approach to government, his rejection of the Western liberal order, and his ability to maintain a regime of absolute power for more than two decades.

Together with Russia, South Africa, Brazil, India, and China, they have formed the BRICS, an alliance for commercial purposes that rivals the hegemony of the US and its allies. Vladimir Putin's discourse focuses on the construction of a multipolar world, where there are no absolute hegemonies, but free trade without fear of arbitrary sanctions.

The future of his regime, and his place in history, will depend on how he handles the economic and political challenges of an increasingly globalized and ever-changing world.

15. Pope Francis

Pope Francis, born Jorge Mario Bergoglio on December 17, 1936, in Buenos Aires, Argentina, became the first Latin American and Jesuit pope when he was elected on March 13, 2013. Since he was elected the 266th pontiff of the Catholic Church, he has been a leader who has marked a new era in the Vatican with a focus on simplicity, social justice, internal Church reform, and interfaith dialogue. His papacy has been notable for its efforts to bring the Church closer to the marginalized, promote mercy, and address global issues such as climate change and economic inequality.

Jorge Mario Bergoglio was born to a family of Italian immigrants in Buenos Aires, where he was raised in a Catholic atmosphere. After completing his secondary education as a chemical technician, Bergoglio felt the call to religious life and joined the Society of Jesus (the Jesuits) in 1958. His religious formation led him to study in seminaries in Argentina and Chile and then to be ordained a priest on December 13, 1969.

Throughout his religious career, Bergoglio was known for his humility, his austere life, and his deep dedication to the poor and marginalized. During the 1970s, while serving as Provincial of the Jesuits in Argentina, he had to navigate the complex and dangerous political climate of the military dictatorship in the country. Although his role in that period has been the subject of debate, Bergoglio has been acknowledged as protecting many from the regime's repression, although he has also been criticized for not taking a more outspoken position against the dictatorship.

In 1998, he was appointed archbishop of Buenos Aires, and in 2001 he was elevated to the rank of cardinal by Pope John Paul II. As archbishop, he distinguished himself by his simplicity and closeness to the people, traveling by public transportation and living in a small apartment instead of the official residence. Bergoglio was known for his pastoral approach, his dedication to the poor, and his staunch opposition to corruption and policies that perpetuated inequality.

The election of Jorge Bergoglio as pope was historic in several ways: he was the first non-European pope in more than 1,200 years, the first Jesuit pope, and the first pontiff to choose the name Francis, in honor of St. Francis of Assisi, the saint of poverty and humility. By taking this name, Bergoglio made it clear that his papacy would focus on the values of simplicity, love for the poor, and care for creation.

From the first moment of his papacy, Pope Francis surprised the world with his direct and humble style. He broke with many papal traditions by renouncing certain symbols of power and luxury, such as the gold cross and the papal throne, preferring an iron cross and living in the Casa Santa Marta, a simple residence instead of the papal palace. These decisions reflected his commitment to a Church closer to the people and less focused on power and prestige.

One of the main challenges that Pope Francis has faced is the reform of the Curia, the Vatican bureaucracy, a key objective since the beginning of his pontificate.

Francis has worked for greater financial transparency in the Vatican, fighting corruption and irregularities within the Vatican Bank. In addition, he has sought to reduce the power of certain conservative sectors within the Church, promoting more inclusive and participatory leadership.

However, one of the greatest challenges of his papacy has been the response to the sexual abuse scandals in the Church. Although Francis has taken steps to address the problem, such as creating commissions for the protection of minors and enacting new accountability laws, his handling of some cases has been criticized, particularly for not acting as quickly or severely as some had hoped at certain times. Nonetheless, Francis has been one of the most outspoken popes in acknowledging the Church's failings and the need for justice for victims.

One of the central themes of Francis' papacy has been his call for social justice and an outgoing Church — that is, a Church that is actively engaged in the world and that stands up for the poorest and most vulnerable. Inspired by the teachings of St. Francis of Assisi, the pope has been a vocal critic of unbridled capitalism, exclusionary globalization, and the throwaway culture, in which the poor, migrants, and the marginalized are ignored.

In his 2013 encyclical "Evangelii Gaudium" (The Joy of the Gospel), Francis stressed the importance of a Church that must be at the service of those in need and denounced economic inequalities. He reiterated his criticism of an economic system that promotes the concentration of wealth and has advocated for a more equitable approach to the distribution of global resources. In this sense, his socialist view of politics has led him to defend regimes of this ideological bent, but without criticizing the cases of corruption or authoritarianism that many present, such as the cases of Venezuela and Argentina.

Another fundamental pillar of Francis' legacy has been his focus on the environment. In 2015, he published his historic encyclical "Laudato si," in which he made an urgent call to care for "our common home." In this document, the Pope connected climate change and environmental degradation with issues of social justice, underscoring how the poor are the most affected by environmental destruction.

"Laudato si" was not only a theological statement but a call to global action to curb global warming, protect ecosystems, and foster sustainable development. In the encyclical, Francis harshly criticized corporations and governments that put economic profits before protecting the planet and called for greater responsibility on the part of developed nations.

Pope Francis has also been a strong advocate of interfaith dialogue and global peace. Since his papacy, he has actively worked to improve relations between the Vatican and other religions, especially with Islam and Judaism. In 2019, he made a historic trip to the United Arab Emirates, where he signed the Document on Human Fraternity alongside the Grand Imam of Al-Azhar, calling for cooperation between Christians and Muslims.

Francis has intervened in several international conflicts, calling for peace in war-torn regions such as Syria and advocating for respect for human rights. In 2014, he played a key role in mediating that helped restore diplomatic relations between the United States and Cuba after decades of hostility.

Despite his global popularity, Francis has faced resistance within the Church, especially from conservative sectors that criticize his pastoral approach, considered by some to be too liberal. Opposition has been expressed around issues such as family, sexuality, and the role of women in the Church. For example, the 2016 apostolic exhortation "Amoris Laetitia," which opened the possibility for some divorced and remarried people to receive communion, was criticized by certain cardinals and theologians, who saw it as a deviation from traditional doctrine.

Likewise, his approach to issues such as gay rights and his call for greater inclusion of migrants has generated controversy among the more traditional sectors of the Church.

Pope Francis' legacy will be remembered for its emphasis on mercy, social justice and integral ecology. He has sought to transform a Church perceived as distant and bureaucratic into an institution closer to the reality of people, especially the poor and marginalized. Under his leadership, the Church has been called to be more inclusive, compassionate, and active in the fight against social and environmental injustices.

Francis is a leader who has sought to balance tradition with the need for reform. While his papacy has faced challenges and resistance, his impact on the way the Church interacts with the world and addresses the great problems of our time will be a fundamental part of his legacy. Through his humility, his call for a "poor Church for the poor" and his courageous stance on global issues, Pope Francis is leaving an indelible mark on the history of Catholicism and the modern world.

16. Jeff Bezos

Jeff Bezos, born Jeffrey Preston Jorgensen on January 12, 1964, in Albuquerque, New Mexico, is the founder of Amazon, one of the largest and most influential technology companies in the world. Through his business vision, innovation, and focus on customer satisfaction, Bezos has transformed retail and revolutionized diverse industries, from technology to media to space exploration. His exercise of power, influence on the global business landscape, and focus on the future have defined his legacy as one of the most important entrepreneurs of the 21st century.

Jeff Bezos was born into a middle-class family. His mother, Jacklyn Gise, was just 17 when she had him, and his biological father, Ted Jorgensen, abandoned the family shortly after Jeff was born. When Bezos was four, his mother married Miguel Bezos, a Cuban immigrant, who adopted Jeff and gave him his last name.

From a young age, Bezos showed a strong inclination towards science and technology. He spent time inventing gadgets and building homemade technology projects. He attended Miami Palmetto Preparatory School and then went on to Princeton University, graduating in 1986 with a bachelor's degree in electrical engineering and computer science.

After graduation, Bezos worked on Wall Street, where he had a successful career at firms such as Bankers Trust and D.E. Shaw, a hedge fund firm where he quickly rose to vice president. However, in 1994, Bezos decided to leave his promising career to pursue a revolutionary idea: selling books over the Internet.

In 1994, Jeff Bezos founded Amazon.com in the garage of his home in Seattle. Originally conceived as an online bookstore, Bezos identified a unique opportunity with the rapid growth of the Internet and the lack of a significant competitor in the e-commerce of books. Bezos' idea was simple but visionary: leverage the scale and global access of the Internet to create a store that could offer more titles than any physical bookstore.

Amazon's launch in 1995 was an immediate success. The company offered a massive catalog of books and soon expanded into other products, starting with music and movies, and then encompassing almost every type of consumer good, from clothing to technology. From the beginning, Bezos placed a strong emphasis on customer satisfaction, a philosophy that would become one of the pillars of Amazon's success.

In the early years, Amazon operated at a loss, as Bezos prioritized growth and expansion over immediate profits. Instead of focusing on short-term profitability, he reinvested revenue into the company's technological infrastructure and improved the customer experience. This strategy, while risky at the time, allowed Amazon to build a loyal customer base and a strong logistics infrastructure.

One of the key decisions that changed Amazon's course was the introduction of Amazon Prime in 2005. For an annual fee, Prime offered free two-day shipping, redefining consumer expectations for fast delivery. This service became a massive success and helped Amazon build even more customer loyalty. Over time, Prime expanded to include additional services such as access to music, TV shows, and movies, cementing Amazon as a major player in the entertainment world.

Prime's success also allowed Amazon to compete more aggressively in retail. The company began offering a vast assortment of consumer products at competitive prices, outperforming many traditional retailers. The expansion of Amazon Marketplace, which allowed third parties to sell products on the platform, further expanded its reach, positioning Amazon as the "one-stop shop" that Bezos had always dreamed of.

Another of Bezos' most visionary decisions was the creation of Amazon Web Services (AWS), launched in 2006. AWS offered cloud services to businesses, allowing them to store and manage data without the need to maintain their servers. This division of Amazon grew rapidly and became one of the most profitable branches of the company, providing services to technology giants such as Netflix, NASA, and many other corporations.

AWS allowed Amazon to diversify its revenue and strengthened Bezos' image as an entrepreneur who not only revolutionized e-commerce but also global technological infrastructure. Today, AWS remains a leader in the cloud computing industry and is one of the main drivers of Amazon's profits.

Jeff Bezos is known for his methodical, data-centric approach, a strategy that has defined his leadership style. At Amazon, he implemented a culture of continuous innovation and experimentation, encouraging his employees to think long-term and not fear failure. His famous 1997 letter to shareholders, where he described Amazon as a "Day 1"-focused company, is emblematic of his philosophy that the company should always maintain a startup mentality, without becoming complacent.

Throughout his career, Bezos has been described as a demanding and perfectionist leader, willing to take big risks to achieve his goals. His ability to anticipate technological trends and his willingness to reinvest profits into new projects have been key to Amazon's continued growth.

Under his leadership, Amazon not only became one of the most valuable companies in the world but also radically changed consumer behavior. His emphasis on convenience, speed, and efficiency transformed customer expectations around the planet and forced competitors like Walmart and Target to adapt or lose ground.

Despite his success at Amazon, Bezos has always had a passion for space. In 2000, he founded Blue Origin, a company dedicated to space exploration, with the vision of making space travel accessible to humanity. Although Blue Origin operated relatively quietly for many years, it has gained notoriety in the past decade with its development of reusable rockets that could make spaceflight more affordable.

Bezos' approach with Blue Origin has been much more long-term than that of rival SpaceX, run by Elon Musk. While SpaceX has focused on government contracts and commercial space missions, Bezos has expressed a desire to establish a long-term, sustainable human presence in space, with the idea that humanity could eventually colonize other planets.

In 2013, Jeff Bezos purchased The Washington Post, one of America's most influential newspapers, for $250 million. His acquisition was viewed with surprise, as Bezos had no prior experience in the media world. However, under his ownership, the Washington Post has experienced a digital renaissance, improved its online presence, and significantly increased its subscriber base.

Bezos has maintained his commitment to not interfering in the newspaper's editorial independence, but his influence has been felt in the technological transformation and expansion of the outlet's digital coverage. The Washington Post has regained relevance in the digital media era and has been an important voice in US political coverage.

Jeff Bezos' legacy is undeniable. He has revolutionized the way we shop, work, and consume content. Under his leadership, Amazon has become a dominant economic force and one of the most influential companies in the world.

However, his rise has not been without controversy. Amazon has been criticized for working conditions at its fulfillment centers, where employees have denounced long hours and demanding work environments. It has also come under fire for its tax practices, with the company exploiting legal loopholes to pay low taxes in several countries.

Bezos has also been criticized for his enormous personal wealth. For years, he was the richest man in the world, reaching a net worth that exceeded $200 billion at one point. His fortune made him a symbol of the growing problem of economic inequality in the world.

Jeff Bezos is one of the most influential entrepreneurs in modern history. His ability to foresee the future of technology and commerce has made him a central figure in the global digital transformation. Through Amazon, Bezos has left an indelible mark on the daily lives of millions of people, changing the way we shop, work, and think about the future.

Despite the controversies and challenges, Bezos' legacy as an innovator and business leader is secure. With his long-term focus, interest in space exploration and impact on diverse industries, Bezos will remain a relevant figure for years to come, both for his business contributions and the social and economic implications of his innovations.

17. Xi Jinping

Xi Jinping, born on June 15, 1953, in Beijing, has been the President of the People's Republic of China since 2013 and General Secretary of the Chinese Communist Party (CCP) since 2012. His leadership has marked a significant change in China's economic, political, and social development. Since coming to power, Xi has consolidated his authority, reformed the military system, intensified party oversight, and projected China as a global power. His authoritarian style of government and focus on restoring China's power and greatness have been fundamental pillars of his legacy.

Xi Jinping comes from an influential family within the Chinese Communist Party. His father, Xi Zhongxun, was one of the founders of the communist guerrilla movement in the 1930s and a veteran revolutionary who held senior government positions, including roles in provincial administration and party leadership. However, during the Cultural Revolution (1966-1976), Xi Zhongxun was purged from the party and imprisoned, which deeply affected Xi Jinping's youth.

During this tumultuous period, Xi Jinping was sent to work in a rural area in Shaanxi province as part of Mao Zedong's efforts to re-educate young urban intellectuals. Despite the difficult conditions, Xi adapted and cultivated relationships with the peasants, gaining a deep understanding of the rural country. These experiences shaped his political outlook and ability to navigate the complexities of power in the Communist Party.

Following Mao's death and the end of the Cultural Revolution, Xi Jinping joined the Chinese Communist Party in 1974. He subsequently studied at Tsinghua University, graduating in chemical engineering in 1979. His rise in the party was gradual, with Xi holding positions in different provinces and standing out for his administrative ability and pragmatic approach.

Xi Jinping rose through the ranks of the Communist Party during the 1980s and 1990s, working at different levels of local government, including in Fujian, Zhejiang, and Shanghai provinces. Throughout his career, Xi earned a reputation as a discreet but effective politician, avoiding scandals and maintaining key relationships within the party.

In 2007, he was promoted to the Politburo Standing Committee, China's most powerful body, positioning him as a strong candidate to succeed President Hu Jintao. In 2012, Xi was elected general secretary of the Communist Party and chairman of the Central Military Commission, and in 2013 he assumed the presidency of China, thereby consolidating his control over the main institutions of power.

One of the most notable features of Xi Jinping's rule has been his ability to consolidate personal power. Unlike his recent predecessors, who retired after two presidential terms, Xi promoted reforms that removed the two-term limit for the president in 2018. This allowed him to stay in power indefinitely and broke with the tradition established after Mao's death, in which Chinese leaders limited their time in office to avoid excessive accumulation of power.

This move was part of a broader process of centralization of power under Xi, which has suppressed any opposition within the party. Through his anti-corruption campaign, Xi has dismissed and punished hundreds of thousands of officials, including senior party officials, in what has been seen as an effort to both clean up the party and eliminate political rivals. This campaign has allowed him to gain control over the military, bureaucracy, and security forces, making him China's most powerful leader since Mao Zedong.

One of Xi Jinping's main ideological contributions has been the promotion of the concept of the "Chinese Dream." This term, coined shortly after his rise to power, reflects Xi's vision of restoring China as a prosperous, strong, and respected global power. The Chinese Dream is articulated around two goals: "socialist modernization" and national rejuvenation, that is, returning China to its central place in world politics.

This goal has been supported by economic policies of sustained growth, the strengthening of military capacity, and a greater presence in international diplomacy. Xi has emphasized the role of socialism with Chinese characteristics as a viable alternative model to Western liberalism, stressing that China can prosper without fully embracing Western-style democracy.

One of the pillars of Xi's leadership has been the reform of the People's Liberation Army (PLA). Under him, Xi has implemented a significant restructuring of the military, reduced the number of troops but increased its technological capacity, and modernized its infrastructure. Military strategy under Xi has placed a strong emphasis on maritime expansion and strengthening China's presence in the South China Sea, leading to tensions with neighboring countries and the United States.

In addition, Xi has promoted a more assertive foreign policy. Through the Belt and Road Initiative, launched in 2013, Xi has sought to expand China's global influence by building infrastructure in more than 60 countries, largely funded by Chinese loans. This project not only seeks to strengthen trade routes but also to expand China's projection of power in strategic regions of Asia, Africa and Europe. The Initiative has been the center of his global strategy, placing China at the heart of the trade routes of the future.

Xi Jinping has used technology extensively to exert greater social and political control over the Chinese population. His government has implemented a system of mass surveillance, including facial recognition cameras, online monitoring, and the development of the social credit system, which ranks citizens based on their behavior and loyalty to the government.

Through strict internet and media regulations, Xi has restricted freedom of expression and consolidated control over the media in China, silencing critics and dissidents. China's Great Firewall has intensified under his leadership, controlling access to outside information and promoting a nationalist narrative within the country.

One of the biggest challenges for Xi Jinping has been the growing resistance in Hong Kong against Beijing's control. Despite the promise of "one country, two systems," which was supposed to guarantee Hong Kong a high degree of autonomy until 2047, Xi's government has increasingly intervened in the region's affairs.

In 2019, mass protests in Hong Kong against a proposed extradition bill to China grew into a broader pro-democracy movement against the Chinese government's increasing control. Xi responded harshly, implementing a National Security Law that severely restricts civil liberties in Hong Kong, further consolidating Beijing's control over the region.

In addition, Xi's government has been criticized internationally for allegations of human rights violations in the autonomous region of Xinjiang, where the government has been accused of mass detentions, forced labor, and political re-education of the Uighur Muslim population. These policies have drawn sanctions and condemnation from several countries, but Xi has maintained his firm stance in defense of China's "internal stability."

Under Xi, China has taken an increasingly assertive stance in international politics, leading to tensions with the United States and other Western countries. During Donald Trump's presidency, China-US relations deteriorated, leading to a trade war that included mutual tariffs and restrictions on technology companies.

Xi has also expanded China's influence in multilateral institutions such as the United Nations, promoting an alternative vision to American leadership on global issues such as climate change, global health, and economic development. However, his aggressive foreign policies, support for authoritarian regimes, and human rights violations have strained China's relations with many democratic countries.

Xi Jinping's legacy is already visible both inside and outside China. Domestically, he has consolidated his control over the Communist Party and positioned China as an economic and military power capable of challenging US hegemony.

18. Henry Kissinger

Henry Alfred Kissinger, born on May 27, 1923, in Fürth, Germany, is one of the most influential figures in the history of international diplomacy and US foreign policy in the 20th century. Of Jewish origin, Kissinger emigrated to the United States in 1938 with his family to escape the Nazi regime and would later become one of the most brilliant strategic minds in world politics.

As national security adviser and Secretary of State under Presidents Richard Nixon and Gerald Ford,

Kissinger played a central role in creating a new era of international relations, marked by détente diplomacy with the Soviet Union, opening to China, and controversy over his role in conflicts such as the Vietnam War and military coups in Latin America. His pragmatic and realistic approach, based on realpolitik, redefined the role of the United States in the world and left a legacy of diplomatic achievements, although not without criticism.

Kissinger was born to a Jewish family in Germany, where he experienced firsthand the increasing anti-Semitic persecution under the Nazi regime. The Kissinger family emigrated to the United States in 1938 and settled in New York. Henry became a naturalized American in 1943 and served in the U.S. Army during World War II, working as an interpreter and in military intelligence because of his fluency in German.

After the war, Kissinger attended Harvard University, where he earned his bachelor's, master's, and doctoral degrees in political science. His doctoral dissertation on 19th-century European politics, titled A World Restored, focusing on the work of Metternich and the balance of power system in Europe, already pointed toward his pragmatic and realist approach to international relations. At Harvard, Kissinger built a strong reputation as a scholar, publishing key works on strategy and geopolitics, which positioned him for a career in government.

Kissinger was recruited by President Richard Nixon in 1969 to serve as national security adviser, a position that placed him at the center of U.S. foreign policy decision-making. Under the Nixon administration,

Kissinger adopted a realpolitik approach, a pragmatic view that favored global stability over ideological considerations, leading him to seek dialogue even with communist regimes, such as the Soviet Union and China.

In 1973, Nixon appointed him Secretary of State, becoming one of the few people in American history to hold both positions at the same time. From this position, Kissinger played a decisive role in the formulation of American foreign policy during one of the most complex periods of the Cold War.

One of Kissinger's most notable achievements was his role in creating the policy of détente with the Soviet Union. Through a balance-of-power and containment approach, Kissinger negotiated several key agreements with Soviet leaders, particularly Leonid Brezhnev. One of the most important was the Strategic Arms Limitation Treaty (SALT I) in 1972, which marked the beginning of a process of nuclear arms control between the two superpowers.

This agreement was instrumental in easing Cold War tensions and preventing an uncontrollable arms race, also earning Kissinger the reputation of a master strategist in global power politics. His ability to understand the complexities of Soviet politics and navigate nuclear diplomacy was a hallmark of his pragmatic and calculating style.

Perhaps Kissinger's most iconic achievement was the historic opening of China. Throughout the Cold War, the United States had isolated Communist China under the leadership of Mao Zedong, but Kissinger saw in the rapprochement with China a strategic opportunity to alter the global balance of power, particularly in the context of tensions between China and the Soviet Union.

In 1971, Kissinger made a secret trip to Beijing that paved the way for Nixon's official visit to China in 1972, an event that marked the reestablishment of diplomatic relations between the two countries and profoundly changed the dynamics of the Cold War. This move not only allowed the United States to establish a closer relationship with an emerging power but also put pressure on the Soviet Union to advance the process of détente.

The reopening of relations with China is widely considered one of the greatest achievements of American diplomacy in the 20th century, and Kissinger was the main architect of this strategic shift.

One of the most controversial episodes in Kissinger's career, however, was his handling of the Vietnam War. From his position as national security adviser, Kissinger was instrumental in formulating the "Vietnamization" strategy, which involved the gradual withdrawal of U.S. troops and the strengthening of the South Vietnamese military to take control of the conflict.

Kissinger was also the lead negotiator of the 1973 Paris Peace Accords, which theoretically ended the war between the United States, North Vietnam, and South Vietnam. For his efforts in negotiating this agreement, Kissinger was awarded the Nobel Peace Prize in 1973, although the war would continue until 1975 when communist forces took Saigon. This situation sparked criticism about the nature of the agreement and the prolongation of the war under his leadership, including the secret bombing of Cambodia and Laos.

Kissinger's foreign policy also had a significant impact in Latin America and Africa, where his interventions generated controversy. In Chile, for example, Kissinger was accused of having actively supported the 1973 military coup that overthrew the democratically elected government of Salvador Allende and led to the dictatorship of Augusto Pinochet. Kissinger justified these actions as necessary to prevent the spread of communism in the Western Hemisphere, although many critics accused him of having contributed to human rights violations.

In Africa, Kissinger intervened in the Angolan conflict, where he supported South African-backed insurgents against the Marxist government. In his African policy, Kissinger sought to limit Soviet and Cuban influence on the continent, but his focus on communist containment often led him to back repressive regimes and perpetuate conflicts.

Henry Kissinger's legacy is deeply complex and polarizing. His defenders see him as a strategic genius who understood the need for a pragmatic approach to foreign policy, guided by national interest and the balance of power. Under his leadership, the United States maintained global stability at a time of great tension and achieved diplomatic breakthroughs that seemed impossible, such as opening to China and arms control with the Soviet Union.

However, his critics accuse him of having prioritized global stability at the expense of human rights and morality. His support for dictatorships and repressive regimes, his involvement in secret wars, and his participation in policies that led to the death and suffering of thousands of people, such as in Vietnam and Chile, have made him a controversial figure. For many, his vision of international politics was excessively cynical and lacking in ethics.

Henry Kissinger remains one of the most influential and debated figures in the history of American foreign policy. His ability to maneuver the complexities of international diplomacy, his role in creating a new global balance during the Cold War, and his pragmatic vision of power have ensured him a central place in modern history. However, his methods and decisions, which often involved serious human rights violations, leave a legacy marked by both success and controversy.

19. Richard Branson

Richard Branson, born on July 18, 1950, in Blackheath, London, is one of the most iconic and innovative entrepreneurs in the world. Founder of the Virgin Group, a multinational conglomerate with interests in industries ranging from music to aviation and space tourism, Branson has revolutionized entire sectors with his bold approach, entrepreneurial spirit, and charismatic personality.

Known for his easy-going style and ability to combine business with showmanship, Branson has become a symbol of innovation and entrepreneurial adventure. His influence has not only redefined industries but has also set a standard for business leadership based on creativity, calculated risk, and a focus on customer experience.

Richard Branson struggled at school due to his dyslexia, which affected his academic performance. Despite these difficulties, from a young age, he showed a strong entrepreneurial instinct. At 16 he left school to find a magazine called Student, which allowed him to connect with a young audience in the 1960s. Although the magazine was not a huge commercial success, Branson had already demonstrated his ability to identify market niches and build businesses based on his intuition.

It was through this early experience that Branson discovered his passion for business and the potential of creating something new from nothing. His next step was to found Virgin Records in 1972, which would mark the true beginning of his career as a global entrepreneur.

Virgin Records, a record company, began as a small record shop in London, which quickly positioned itself as an innovative label, signing artists that other, more conventional labels considered risky. One of Virgin's first big hits was Mike Oldfield's album Tubular Bells, which became a global phenomenon.

During the 1970s and 1980s, Virgin Records signed some of the most influential artists of the time, including the Sex Pistols, Culture Club, and The Rolling Stones. Branson was noted for his ability to spot talent in emerging genres and for taking risks that other industry executives avoided. Under his leadership, Virgin Records became one of the most important record labels in the world, transforming the music landscape of the time.

However, in 1992, in a strategic move to save other areas of his business empire, Branson sold Virgin Records to EMI for approximately $1 billion. Although it was a painful decision for him, this sale allowed him to focus on other areas of his Virgin empire.

One of the most notable aspects of Richard Branson's business legacy is his ability to diversify his empire and bring the Virgin brand to a wide range of industries. Following the success of Virgin Records, Branson launched Virgin Atlantic in 1984, his foray into the airline industry. Virgin Atlantic stood out from the start for its focus on customer service and innovation, challenging industry giants like British Airways. The airline pioneered amenities that would become standard, such as more spacious seats and in-flight entertainment.

The creation of Virgin Atlantic was a testament to Branson's leadership style, based on the idea that customer experience should be the primary focus. His decision to enter an industry as regulated and competitive as aviation was seen as risky, but it turned out to be a successful move that cemented his reputation as an entrepreneur willing to challenge the status quo.

Over the years, Branson continued to expand the Virgin Group into other industries, such as rail transport (Virgin Trains), telecommunications (Virgin Mobile), healthcare (Virgin Health) and financial services (Virgin Money). Each of these forays was marked by Branson's signature strategy: challenging established players through innovation and a fresh, consumer-focused approach.

Richard Branson's adventurous spirit goes beyond business. Throughout his life, he has undertaken numerous record-breaking challenges, including attempts to circumnavigate the world in hot air balloons and on boats, which has cemented his image as a global adventurer. These challenges have served both to generate publicity for his brands and to satisfy his desire for adventure and risk.

His approach to business and personal life has been characterized by a strong rejection of conformity and a penchant for embracing failure as an opportunity to learn. Branson has spoken openly about his entrepreneurial mistakes, including failed attempts at Virgin Cola (to compete against Coca-Cola) and Virgin Brides (a wedding dress business), which humanizes him as an entrepreneur and shows his resilience in the face of adversity.

One of Branson's most ambitious and revolutionary projects is Virgin Galactic, a company founded in 2004 to make space travel accessible to the public. Virgin Galactic represents one of the biggest and riskiest bets in the commercial space race, to take tourists into space on suborbital flights.

This project is part of Branson's long-term vision to create an entirely new space tourism industry, which could fundamentally change humans' relationship with outer space. Although there have been multiple delays and technical challenges, in 2021 Virgin Galactic conducted its first manned space flight, with Branson on board, demonstrating his commitment to the project.

Despite the challenges and criticism, Virgin Galactic symbolizes Branson's visionary entrepreneurial spirit, which is willing to take risks at the frontier of innovation.

Branson is not only known for his business success but also for his philanthropy and social activism. In 2004, he founded Virgin Unite, the Virgin Group's non-profit foundation dedicated to addressing global challenges such as poverty, climate change, and human rights. Through this organization, Branson has worked on social impact initiatives and has collaborated with other prominent figures, such as Nelson Mandela and Desmond Tutu, in the creation of The Elders, an organization of world leaders that seeks to promote peace and human rights.

Branson has also been a strong advocate for action against climate change and has invested in renewable energy technologies. His Carbon War Room project is designed to identify and accelerate business solutions to reduce carbon emissions globally.

Throughout his life, Branson has promoted a business philosophy that combines financial success with a conscious approach to social and environmental impact. This approach has influenced a new generation of entrepreneurs, who see Branson as a model for how business can be a driver of positive change.

Richard Branson's leadership style is notable for its decentralized approach and emphasis on business culture. Branson is known for delegating power to his teams and fostering a relaxed and creative work environment. His non-hierarchical style has inspired many business leaders to adopt more flexible management models and place greater emphasis on employee and customer satisfaction.

In addition, his charisma and ability to generate close personal relationships with employees, business partners, and the public have given him a unique competitive advantage in the business world. Branson has proven that the power of a personal brand when combined with a strong business vision, can be a driving force in the success of a business.

Richard Branson has left an indelible mark on the business world and popular culture. As the founder of Virgin, he has created one of the most diverse and innovative business empires in the world. His bold approach, ability to identify new market opportunities, and approachable and empathetic leadership style have made him a global icon.

Despite some failures and setbacks, his legacy is that of a tireless visionary who has redefined what it means to be an entrepreneur in the 21st century. With initiatives such as Virgin Galactic, Branson continues to look to the future, proving that his ability to dream big and take calculated risks remains a central part of his legacy.

His holistic approach, combining financial success with social and environmental awareness, has set a new standard for business leaders, and his influence will continue to shape the future of global innovation and entrepreneurship.

20. Fidel Castro

Fidel Alejandro Castro Ruz, born on August 13, 1926, in Birán, Cuba, was one of the most influential and controversial political figures of the 20th century. Leader of the Cuban Revolution and president of Cuba for nearly five decades, Castro left a profound mark on global political history and that of Latin America, confronting the power of the United States and leading one of the few communist governments in the Western Hemisphere.

Under his leadership, Cuba underwent profound social, economic, and political transformations. However, his rule was also marked by repression, a lack of civil liberties, and human rights abuses, generating strong criticism. Castro was admired by some for his resistance to imperialism and his fight for Cuban sovereignty, while others saw him as a dictator who kept his country in poverty and isolation.

Fidel Castro was born to a well-off family in Birán, in the province of Oriente, Cuba. His father, Ángel Castro, was a Spanish immigrant who had prospered in agriculture. Despite his privileged background, Castro showed an interest in politics and social justice from a young age. He studied at Jesuit schools before entering the University of Havana, where he studied law. It was at the university that he began his political career, participating in student protest movements and becoming increasingly critical of the Cuban regime under dictator Fulgencio Batista.

During these years, Castro developed a mix of nationalist and Marxist ideals, convinced that US imperialism was responsible for many of the problems of Cuba and Latin America. In 1953, aged just 26, he led a failed attack on the Moncada military barracks in Santiago de Cuba, leading to his arrest and subsequent exile. However, his famous statement at the trial, "History will absolve me," cemented him as a figure of resistance in the Cuban imagination.

Following his release in 1955, Castro went into exile in Mexico, where he organized a small group of revolutionaries that included his brother Raúl Castro and Argentine Ernesto "Che" Guevara. In 1956, these men landed in Cuba aboard the Granma to begin a guerrilla campaign against the Batista regime. Although they were initially hunted down and nearly wiped out, Castro and his forces managed to establish a base of operations in the Sierra Maestra mountains.

As the guerrillas advanced, the revolutionary movement gained strength and popular support, especially among peasants and the poorer classes, dissatisfied with the corruption and repression of the Batista regime. In 1959, Batista fled the country, and Castro triumphantly entered Havana. The Cuban Revolution was a radical change in Cuban politics and laid the groundwork for the establishment of a socialist state.

Following the revolutionary victory, Fidel Castro quickly consolidated his control over the new Cuban government. At first, he did not openly define himself as a communist, but in the following years, he allied himself closely with the Soviet Union and declared Cuba a Marxist-Leninist state. This decision had profound implications for Cuban foreign policy and economy.

Under Castro's authority, the government expropriated private lands and businesses, much of it American-owned, and nationalized banking and industry. This led to a rapid break in relations with the United States, which imposed an economic embargo on Cuba in 1960. In response, Castro consolidated his alliance with the Soviet Union, which guaranteed Moscow's financial and military support for decades.

Castro's leadership was marked by the centralization of power. In 1965, he founded the Cuban Communist Party and in 1976 he officially assumed the titles of President of the Council of State and President of the Council of Ministers, giving him control over all aspects of Cuba's political, military, and economic life.

One of the tensest moments in the history of the Cold War and Castro's presidency was the Cuban Missile Crisis of 1962. In response to the failed CIA-backed

Bay of Pigs invasion of 1961 and the face of continued US hostility, Castro allowed the installation of Soviet nuclear missiles on Cuban territory, sparking a confrontation between the United States and the Soviet Union.

U.S. President John F. Kennedy and Soviet leader Nikita Khrushchev negotiated the removal of the missiles in exchange for the United States not invading Cuba, but Castro felt betrayed by Khrushchev for not having been consulted in the negotiations. The crisis elevated Castro to the international stage as a key figure in the Cold War and cemented his reputation as a defiant and uncompromising leader in the face of the superpowers.

Domestically, Castro's government carried out a series of social and economic reforms that profoundly changed the structure of Cuban society. It implemented massive literacy programs and significantly improved access to public health care, leading Cuba to achieve some of the best health and education indicators in Latin America. The elimination of major economic inequalities was one of the key achievements of the Revolution.

However, these social advances came at a high cost. The Cuban economy, highly dependent on sugar and exports, suffered under centralized control and a lack of innovation. In addition, the US embargo and reliance on Soviet subsidies left the country in a precarious economic situation. With the fall of the Soviet Union in 1991, Cuba entered the "Special Period," a severe economic crisis that plunged the country into extreme poverty.

Fidel Castro consolidated his power not only through his social reforms but also through strict political control. His government was repeatedly accused of human rights violations, including repressing press freedom, censoring dissent, and imprisoning political opponents. Dissidents were jailed or forced into exile, and the media and cultural institutions were tightly controlled by the state.

The lack of civil and political liberties was a constant under his rule, leading many to condemn his regime as a dictatorship. However, Castro was also celebrated for maintaining Cuba's independence from US imperialism and for offering support to revolutionary movements in Latin America, Africa, and elsewhere around the world.

Internationally, Fidel Castro became a symbol of anti-imperialism and the global communist movement. Under his leadership, Cuba supported liberation movements in Latin America and Africa. In Angola, for example, Cuban troops played a key role in the country's independence from Portuguese colonial rule, and in the Congo and Ethiopia, Cuba also supported revolutionary movements.

Castro was a central figure in the Non-Aligned Movement, a coalition of nations that did not want to align themselves with either the United States or the Soviet Union during the Cold War. This position allowed him to cultivate relationships with countries in Africa, Asia, and the Middle East, despite tensions with the West.

In 2006, after nearly 50 years as the head of the Cuban government, Fidel Castro provisionally handed over power to his brother Raúl Castro due to health problems. In 2008, Raúl officially assumed the presidency, marking the end of an era. Despite his retirement, Fidel continued to influence Cuban politics through his publications and speeches.

Fidel Castro died on November 25, 2016, at the age of 90, leaving behind a deeply divisive legacy. To some, he was a revolutionary hero who challenged imperialism and fought for social equality. To others, he was a dictator who repressed his people and led his country to economic ruin.

Fidel Castro's legacy is complex and deeply polarizing. His achievements in health, and education, and his commitment to fighting imperialism made him a respected figure in many Third World countries. To his critics, however, Castro was a dictator who ruled with an iron fist, eliminating political freedoms and condemning his country to decades of poverty and isolation. The US economic embargo, coupled with economic mismanagement and a lack of reforms, meant that many Cubans suffered during his rule.

Fidel Castro's name will continue to be synonymous with revolution, resistance, and controversy. Despite the deep divisions his figure provoked, there is no doubt that Castro was one of the most influential leaders of the 20th century, leaving an indelible mark both in Cuba and on the global political stage.

21. Vladimir Lenin

Vladimir Ilyich Ulyanov, better known as Vladimir Lenin, was one of the most influential political leaders of the 20th century. Born on April 22, 1870, in Simbirsk, Russia, Lenin was the architect of the Bolshevik Revolution of 1917 and the principal founder of the Soviet Union. His revolutionary ideas based on Marxism and his leadership in consolidating the world's first socialist state left an indelible mark on global history.

Through his leadership of the October Revolution, Lenin not only transformed Russia but also inspired communist movements around the world. Despite his early death in 1924, his legacy and influence continue to be debated, both for his role in creating a new political system and the consequences of the repressive policies that followed under Stalinism.

Vladimir Lenin was born into a well-off family. His father was a school inspector, which allowed Lenin to access a quality education from an early age. Lenin's life changed radically in 1887, when his elder brother, Aleksandr Ulyanov, was executed for participating in a plot to assassinate Tsar Alexander III. His brother's death radicalized Lenin and propelled him toward revolutionary politics.

Lenin studied law at Kazan University but was expelled soon after for participating in political activities. From that point on, he began to become deeply involved in Marxism, influenced by the works of Karl Marx and Friedrich Engels. He moved to St. Petersburg, where he joined socialist circles and engaged in the underground organization of revolutionary movements.

Because of his revolutionary activities, Lenin was arrested and exiled to Siberia in 1897. During his exile, he wrote extensively on politics and economics and began to develop his ideas on Marxism adapted to the specific conditions of Russia. In 1900, after his release, he moved to Western Europe, where he spent most of the next 17 years in exile, writing and organizing the revolutionary struggle from abroad.

In 1903, Lenin led the split within the Russian Social Democratic Workers' Party, which split into two factions: the Bolsheviks, which Lenin led and who advocated an immediate revolution and a dictatorship of the proletariat, and the Mensheviks, who advocated a more gradual path to socialism. This split was key in the future history of the party and Russian socialism, as the Bolsheviks would eventually take control under Lenin's leadership.

Lenin developed his theory on the need for a vanguard party made up of professional revolutionaries who would lead the working class toward socialism. This theory, which departed from classical Marxism, would be one of the keys to understanding the success of Bolshevism in Russia.

The year 1917 was a decisive one in Lenin's life and the history of Russia. The First World War devastated the country, creating a deep political, economic, and social crisis. In February of that year, a popular revolution overthrew Tsar Nicholas II and established a provisional government. However, this new government kept Russia in the war, which generated growing discontent among the masses.

Lenin, who was in exile in Switzerland, saw in this situation the perfect opportunity for a socialist revolution. With the help of Germany, which hoped that his return would destabilize Russia, Lenin returned to the country in April 1917. Upon arrival, he published his famous "April Theses," in which he argued for the need to overthrow the provisional government, withdraw Russia from the war, and transfer all power to the Soviets, councils made up of workers, soldiers, and peasants.

In October 1917, the Bolsheviks, under the leadership of Lenin and Leon Trotsky, led the October Revolution, which overthrew the provisional government in a nearly bloodless coup. Lenin assumed control of the government and began implementing radical policies to transform Russia into a socialist state.

Following the October Revolution, Lenin faced fierce opposition both internally and externally. In 1918, a civil war broke out between the Red Army, loyal to the Bolsheviks, and the White Army, made up of various counter-revolutionary forces. During this period, Lenin took extreme measures to maintain power and consolidate the new Soviet state.

One of Lenin's most controversial policies during the Civil War was War Communism, which included the nationalization of industry and the forced confiscation of food from peasants to supply the army and cities. These policies, while necessary for the survival of the

Bolshevik regime, led to massive famine and widespread discontent in rural areas.

In parallel, Lenin launched a campaign of repression against his political enemies, using the Cheka, the Bolshevik secret police, to eliminate any opposition. This repression, known as the Red Terror, laid the groundwork for the future purges and abuses that would characterize the Soviet regime, especially under the leadership of Joseph Stalin.

In 1922, the civil war ended with the victory of the Red Army and the consolidation of Bolshevik power in most of the former Russian Empire. That same year, the Union of Soviet Socialist Republics (USSR) was founded, with Lenin as its undisputed leader. However, the country was devastated by war, famine, and deindustrialization.

To deal with the economic crisis, Lenin introduced the New Economic Policy (NEP) in 1921, a temporary measure that allowed a limited degree of private ownership and free markets, especially in agriculture and trade. The NEP was a pragmatic recognition that War Communism had failed and that a more flexible approach was needed to rebuild the economy.

Although the NEP helped stabilize the economy, Lenin always considered it a temporary solution and hoped that the country would eventually return to fully socialist economic planning.

Beginning in 1922, Lenin's health began to deteriorate, affected by a series of strokes that left him partially paralyzed and unable to actively govern. During his later years, Lenin became concerned about the growing power of Joseph Stalin, who had risen to key positions within the Communist Party. In his Testament, Lenin recommended Stalin's dismissal from the post of General Secretary, warning that his authoritarian character was dangerous to the future of socialism. However, this recommendation was ignored following Lenin's death.

Lenin died on January 21, 1924. His body was embalmed and placed in a mausoleum in Moscow's Red Square, where it remains to this day. Lenin's death marked the end of an era, but the state he had created, the Soviet Union, would endure until its collapse in 1991. Upon his death, a fierce power struggle broke out, eventually leading to Stalin consolidating himself as the absolute leader of the party and the country.

Vladimir Lenin's legacy is monumental and deeply complex. As the leader of history's first successful socialist revolution, Lenin inspired generations of communists and revolutionaries around the world. His vision of a socialist state and his interpretation of Marxism, known as Leninism, became the ideological foundation for numerous revolutionary movements in Latin America, Asia, and Africa.

Lenin is seen by many as a brilliant strategist and a pragmatic leader who knew how to adapt to circumstances to carry out his revolutionary vision. However, his use of violence, repression, and the establishment of a one-party state laid the groundwork for the abuses that would come later, particularly under Stalin's leadership.

Leninism, which advocates a revolutionary vanguard party and the dictatorship of the proletariat, has been criticized by those who see in it the seeds of Soviet authoritarianism. Despite this, Lenin's influence lives on in many left-wing movements who see his fight for workers' emancipation and social justice as an example to follow.

Vladimir Lenin was, without a doubt, one of the most influential figures of the 20th century. As the leader of the Bolshevik Revolution and founder of the Soviet Union, Lenin changed the course of world history. His life and work continue to be the subject of debate, both for his contributions to political theory and for the consequences of the policies he implemented. His legacy, for better or worse, lives on in the contemporary world.

22. Mark Zuckerberg

Mark Zuckerberg, co-founder and current CEO of Meta Platforms, formerly known as Facebook, is one of the most influential and controversial figures in the world of technology and business. Born on May 14, 1984, in White Plains, New York, Zuckerberg revolutionized the way people connect and communicate over the internet. Since launching Facebook in 2004, its platform has grown to become one of the largest and most powerful companies in the world, with billions of users.

While Zuckerberg has been praised for his vision and ability to transform digital interaction, he has also faced numerous criticisms, both for the way he handles user privacy and for Facebook's role in spreading misinformation and harmful content. His influence, both in the technological social, and political spheres, has left a legacy that continues to shape the future of communications and technology.

Zuckerberg showed an early aptitude for computer science. Raised in an upper-middle-class Jewish family, his education and skills were fostered by his father, a dentist, and his mother, a psychiatrist. From an early age, Mark excelled at computer programming, creating his first programs at a very early age. During his teens, he designed a program called ZuckNet, a simple communication tool that his father used for his dental office.

Zuckerberg attended the prestigious Phillips Exeter Academy before enrolling at Harvard in 2002, where he initially studied psychology and computer science. At Harvard, he began developing several projects, including Facemash, a platform that allowed students to compare photos of fellow students and vote on who was most attractive. This project, although controversial and quickly shut down by the university, was the precursor to what would become Facebook.

In 2004, together with fellow students Eduardo Saverin, Andrew McCollum, Dustin Moskovitz, and Chris Hughes, Zuckerberg launched "Facebook," a social network initially limited to Harvard students. The idea was simple: create a space where students could interact, share photos, and keep up with their peers' activities.

Success was instant, and Zuckerberg quickly expanded the platform to other American universities. Facebook's popularity grew exponentially, and before long, Zuckerberg dropped out of Harvard to devote himself entirely to developing the platform. In 2005, he received his first major investment from Peter Thiel, co-founder of PayPal, allowing for the site's massive expansion.

Now based in Palo Alto, California, Zuckerberg transformed Facebook into a global platform. In 2006, the social network was opened to anyone over the age of 13 with a valid email address, marking the start of its explosive growth.

As Facebook grew, Zuckerberg consolidated his control over the company. Unlike other tech giants of his time, Zuckerberg has always held a large amount of voting stock, allowing him to maintain almost absolute control over the company's strategic and operational decisions. This control has been instrumental in carrying out his vision of transforming Facebook into a central platform for the digital lives of millions of people.

Facebook continued to expand, buying other key platforms such as Instagram in 2012 and WhatsApp in 2014, helping Zuckerberg consolidate his dominance in the social media space. Under his leadership, Facebook not only became the most popular social network in the world but also transformed into a giant advertising platform, competing with Google for the largest share of the digital advertising market.

However, throughout his career, Zuckerberg has faced significant challenges. The company has come under intense criticism for the way it handles user data, as well as its role in spreading fake news, political propaganda, and divisive content. In particular, the Cambridge Analytica scandal in 2018, in which it was revealed that the data of millions of users had been used without their consent to influence political elections, shook the company's reputation and placed Zuckerberg at the center of discussions about privacy in the digital age.

In 2021, Zuckerberg announced the change of the company's name from Facebook Inc. to Meta Platforms Inc., reflecting his ambition to lead the development of the metaverse, a vision of an immersive, three-dimensional internet where people interact in virtual environments. This change marks a new phase in Zuckerberg's journey as a technology visionary, who sees the metaverse as the future of social, work, and recreational interactions.

Although the metaverse project is still in development, Zuckerberg has invested billions of dollars in research and development in this area, including the creation of hardware such as the Oculus virtual reality headset. Despite the skepticism surrounding this bet, Zuckerberg is convinced that the metaverse will redefine the way people connect and work, just as Facebook did in its time.

Mark Zuckerberg's legacy is closely linked to his ability to transform the way people interact online. With more than 3 billion users across his various platforms (Facebook, Instagram, WhatsApp), he has changed the landscape of global communications and digital advertising, creating an empire that transcends borders.

Under his leadership, Facebook has grown from a university social network to a global digital ecosystem that influences all aspects of modern life, from personal communication to political activism. However, with this power has come great responsibility and a series of ethical and social challenges. Zuckerberg has been heavily criticized for his handling of misinformation, hate speech, and user privacy, leading some to question whether his focus on growth and corporate power has had negative consequences for society.

On the other hand, Zuckerberg has used his fortune for philanthropy. Together with his wife, Priscilla Chan, he founded the Chan Zuckerberg Initiative, dedicated to education, healthcare, and scientific research. Through this organization, he has pledged to donate a significant portion of his wealth to address some of the world's most pressing problems, such as eradicating disease and improving access to education.

Mark Zuckerberg has left a profound mark on the modern world. As the founder of Facebook and leader of Meta, he has transformed the way people interact, communicate, and consume information online. His innovative vision, his ability to maintain control of one of the world's largest companies, and his ambition to lead the next technological revolution with the metaverse have cemented his place as one of the most influential entrepreneurs of the 21st century.

Despite the controversies that have marked his career, Zuckerberg has redefined the digital age. His influence remains immense and his legacy, though complex, continues to evolve as his company seeks new technological frontiers.

23. Karl Marx

Karl Heinrich Marx (1818-1883) was a German philosopher, economist, historian, sociologist, and journalist whose ideas have profoundly shaped the political and social history of the world. He is widely known for being the co-author, with Friedrich Engels, of the Communist Manifesto and the author of Capital, two of the most influential texts in political and economic theory. Marx is the father of Marxism, a doctrine that advocates class struggle and the establishment of a classless, exploitation-free society, which has inspired numerous revolutionary movements and the creation of socialist states around the world.

Although Marx was not a politician in the practical sense of directly exercising power, his ideas have had a massive impact on shaping the political and economic structures of the 20th century. Through his critique of capitalism and his proposal for a communist society, Marx not only influenced the revolutions of countries such as Russia, China, and Cuba but also left an intellectual legacy that remains relevant in contemporary debates about inequality and social justice.

Karl Marx was born on 5 May 1818 in Trier, in what is now Germany, to a Jewish family who later converted to Lutheranism. His father, a lawyer, encouraged him to pursue an academic career, and Marx studied at the universities of Bonn and Berlin, where he became deeply interested in Hegelian philosophy. It was in Berlin that Marx joined a group of radical Young Hegelians who questioned the conservative Prussian system and advocated political reforms.

During his university studies, Marx distanced himself from classical Hegelian thought, developing a materialist critique of history and society. Influenced by Ludwig Feuerbach, he began to move away from Hegelian metaphysics and focus on more practical, earthly issues, such as economics and power relations in society. This intellectual evolution would be crucial to the development of his theory of historical materialism, which states that economic structures are the foundation upon which all political and social institutions are built.

In 1843, Marx moved to Paris, where he met Friedrich Engels, who would become his closest collaborator. Engels had written about the conditions of workers in England, and his ideas about the exploitation of the working class resonated with Marx's concerns about capitalism. Together, they began working on formulating what would later become known as

Marxism, a theory combining a radical critique of capitalism with a vision of a future classless society.

In 1848, Marx and Engels published the Communist Manifesto, one of the most influential political texts in history. In this document, Marx and Engels laid out their theory of class struggle, stating that the history of all societies thus far was the history of the struggle between the ruling and oppressed classes. According to Marx, modern capitalism had generated a new exploited class, the proletariat, which would eventually rise to overthrow the bourgeoisie and establish a communist society.

The Communist Manifesto had an immediate impact, as it was published in a context of revolutionary upheaval in Europe, especially in 1848, when revolutions broke out in several European countries. Although these uprisings were suppressed, the Manifesto served as an ideological roadmap for the workers' movements of the following decades.

After the failure of the 1848 revolutions, Marx went into exile in London, where he would spend the rest of his life. Although he lived in difficult economic conditions, often dependent on Engels' financial support, Marx continued his theoretical work. During this period, he wrote his magnum opus, Capital. The first of its three parts was published in 1867, while the other two were compiled posthumously by Engels.

In Capital, Marx develops his most profound and systematic critique of capitalism, analyzing the nature of the commodity, the accumulation of capital, and the exploitation of the working class through surplus value. Marx argued that capitalism is inherently unstable and self-destructive due to internal contradictions between productive forces and relations of production. According to Marx, the capitalist system would inevitably lead to recurring economic crises, polarization between rich and poor, and ultimately, proletarian revolution.

This detailed analysis of the capitalist economy was a key contribution not only to socialist theory but also to political economy and sociology. Although Capital was not widely recognized in its time, over the decades it would become a fundamental reference for economists critical of capitalism and for revolutionary movements around the world.

Although Karl Marx did not live to see the triumph of his ideas in practice, his influence grew significantly after he died in 1883. During the 20th century, Marxism became the ideological basis for numerous communist revolutions and movements. The Russian Revolution of 1917, led by Vladimir Lenin, was perhaps the most prominent example of the application of Marx's ideas to a concrete situation. Lenin adapted Marx's theories to justify a dictatorship of the proletariat and the establishment of a socialist state.

The success of the Russian Revolution was followed by a series of communist revolutions around the world, such as in China under Mao Zedong and in Cuba under Fidel Castro. Although these leaders adapted Marxism to the specific conditions of their respective countries, they were all based on Marx's fundamental ideas about class struggle and the need to overthrow capitalism.

Marx's legacy was also manifested in the rise of communist and socialist parties in Europe and Latin America, many of which played key roles in the politics of their respective countries. Furthermore, during the Cold War, the confrontation between the communist bloc led by the Soviet Union and Western capitalist democracies reflected the profound impact of Marx's ideas on global geopolitics.

Beyond his direct influence on revolutionary movements, Marx's legacy as a thinker and theorist remains relevant in contemporary debates on economics, politics, and sociology. Marxism has been the subject of numerous reinterpretations and critiques, but its fundamental insights into inequality, exploitation, and the inherent contradictions of capitalism continue to resonate in the 21st century.

Marx predicted that capitalism would generate increasing polarization between the capitalist class and workers, a phenomenon that many contemporary observers associate with rising economic inequality and the concentration of wealth in the hands of a few global corporations. Furthermore, his critique of commodity fetishism and the alienation of workers in the capitalist system has been widely discussed by theorists in fields such as economics, sociology, and psychology.

Marx's analysis of the dynamics of power and exploitation remains a critical tool for those seeking to understand the recurring economic crises and social tensions in contemporary capitalist societies. Although state socialism in countries such as the USSR collapsed, left-wing movements around the world continue to use Marx's work as a basis for their analyses and proposals.

Karl Marx is, without a doubt, one of the most influential figures in intellectual and political history. His critique of capitalism and his vision of a communist society have inspired revolutions, social movements, and governments throughout the 20th century. Even though his ideas were applied in diverse and often controversial ways, his legacy remains profound and relevant.

Marx not only changed the course of political theory but also helped define the terms of the debate over social justice, exploitation, and economic power that remain relevant today. His writings, especially Capital and the Communist Manifesto, continue to be fundamental for those seeking to understand and critique the economic and political structures that dominate the world today.

24. Sigmund Freud

Sigmund Freud (1856-1939) is one of the most influential figures of the 20th century and the founder of psychoanalysis, a revolutionary theory of the unconscious that has transformed our understanding of the human mind. Freud not only introduced fundamental concepts such as the unconscious, defense mechanisms, and transference but also proposed a new way of understanding human development, especially through his theory of infantile sexuality and the Oedipus complex. Through his work, Freud changed the way psychotherapy, mental disorders, and the nature of the human being are conceived.

Although his theories have been the subject of controversy and criticism, Freud's influence is undeniable, both in psychology and in disciplines as diverse as philosophy, literature, and social sciences.

Sigismund Schlomo Freud was born on May 6, 1856, in Freiberg, Moravia (today Příbor, in the Czech Republic), to a middle-class Jewish family. When Freud was four years old, his family moved to Vienna, where he would spend most of his life. From a young age, Freud showed great intellectual ability, excelling in school and showing interest in science and thought.

Freud studied medicine at the University of Vienna, where he was a student of several influential scientists, including Ernst Brücke, who held a materialistic view of the mind. Under this influence, Freud began to develop a scientific conception of the brain and human behavior. Although he began his career as a general physician and neurologist, his real interest was in understanding the human mind, especially mental disorders.

In 1885, Freud traveled to Paris to study with Jean-Martin Charcot, a neurologist who used hypnosis to treat hysteria. Charcot deeply influenced Freud by showing him that hysterical symptoms, such as paralysis and fainting, could have psychological causes, leading him to conclude that mental illness did not always have a physical basis.

Freud's return to Vienna marked the beginning of his pioneering work in psychotherapy. He began collaborating with Josef Breuer, who was using the cathartic method, that is, allowing patients to recall and verbalize traumatic experiences, which alleviated their symptoms. Freud and Breuer together published the influential book "Studies on Hysteria" (1895), which laid the groundwork for the development of psychoanalysis.

One of Freud's major contributions was the formulation of his theory of the unconscious. Freud observed that many repressed experiences and desires influenced people's behavior, often unconsciously. Through his work with patients, Freud developed the method of free association, where the patient spoke uncensored about whatever came to mind, allowing repressed thoughts to be accessed. This was crucial to the birth of psychoanalysis as a therapeutic and theoretical tool.

Freud's concept of the unconscious was one of the most important innovations in modern psychology. Freud proposed that the human mind was divided into three parts: the conscious, the preconscious, and the unconscious. According to Freud, the unconscious housed repressed memories, desires, and emotions that influence people's behavior and conscious thoughts, often causing internal conflicts.

Freud is also famous for his analysis of dreams, which he saw as the "royal road" to the unconscious. In his work "The Interpretation of Dreams" (1900), Freud explained that dreams are disguised expressions of repressed desires. He used dream analysis as a key tool in his therapeutic practice to unravel his patients' internal conflicts.

One of Freud's most controversial theories is his conception of childhood sexuality. Freud held that sexual drives do not emerge only at puberty but are present from birth and evolve through various stages of development. He defined stages of psychosexual development such as the oral, anal, and phallic phases, each of which is related to an area of the body that pleasures each stage.

The Oedipus complex is perhaps the best-known part of his theory of infantile sexuality. Freud proposed that, during the phallic phase, children experience an unconscious desire for the opposite-sex parent and feelings of rivalry with the same-sex parent. This concept has been highly debated but remains one of the cornerstones of his theory.

Throughout his career, Freud refined his model of the mind. He proposed that the human personality was structured into three components: the id, the ego, and the superego. The id represents instinctive and primitive desires, the superego is the internalization of social and moral norms, and the ego acts as a mediator between the two, seeking to satisfy the desires of the id in a socially acceptable way. This theory of internal psychic conflict has been central to Freud's understanding of human behavior.

Freud was not only powerful in terms of his intellectual influence but also in building a psychoanalytic movement that changed the practice of psychotherapy. In 1902, Freud was appointed extraordinary professor at the University of Vienna, an important, if belated, recognition of his contribution to science. That same year, he founded the Vienna Psychoanalytic Society, where leading disciples, such as Carl Jung and Alfred Adler, met to discuss and disseminate their theories. These meetings helped establish psychoanalysis as a formal field and expand its influence beyond Austria.

Throughout his life, Freud was a controversial figure, challenging traditional conceptions of the mind and morality of his day. Despite initial resistance from the medical and academic community, the power of Freud's ideas was expanding, especially in Europe and North America. Several of his disciples, such as Jung and Adler, developed their schools of thought, divergent from Freudian teachings, underscoring the multifaceted impact he had on modern psychology.

In 1938, after the Nazis annexed Austria, Freud, who was Jewish, fled Vienna to London with his family. He was already suffering from cancer of the jaw, an illness that plagued him during the last years of his life. He died in London on September 23, 1939, aged 83.

Despite the controversy that has surrounded many of his ideas, Freud's legacy is immense. Psychoanalysis has had a profound influence not only on psychology and psychiatry but also on areas such as literature, philosophy, film, and art. Freudian ideas about the unconscious, repression, and sexuality have permeated popular culture and continue to be the subject of study and debate.

Psychoanalysis as a therapeutic practice continues to be used in many parts of the world, most notably in Argentina and France, although it has been supplemented and, in some cases, replaced by more modern psychological approaches, such as cognitive-behavioral therapy. However, Freud's focus on the importance of internal conflicts, unconscious desires, and childhood in the formation of personality remains a fundamental basis for many forms of psychological therapy.

Freud's influence transcends the clinical and academic realm. His theories have influenced art, film, literature, and cultural criticism. Authors and filmmakers from James Joyce to Luis Buñuel have used Freudian concepts to explore the darker corners of the human mind. In addition, Freud's theory on dreams, sexuality, and defense mechanisms has provided a framework for interpreting human behavior in a variety of contexts.

Freud has also been the subject of intense criticism, however. Some critics claim that his theories lack scientific rigor and that many of his clinical cases were interpreted subjectively. Others have pointed out that his theories, particularly his focus on childhood sexuality and the Oedipus complex, are reductionist and not applicable to all cultures. Despite these criticisms, Freud's importance in the history of thought remains indisputable.

25. Albert Einstein

Albert Einstein (1879-1955) is widely recognized as one of the greatest scientists in history, and his name is synonymous with genius. Einstein's most celebrated contribution is his theory of relativity, which revolutionized the understanding of fundamental concepts such as space, time, energy, and gravity. His famous equation $E=mc^2$, which describes the equivalence between mass and energy, had a profound impact on both theoretical science and practical applications, such as the development of nuclear energy.

Throughout his life, Einstein was not only an exceptional physicist, but also a public figure who used his influence to promote peace and social justice.

Albert Einstein was born on March 14, 1879, in Ulm, in the Kingdom of Württemberg (Germany). Although his family was Jewish, they were not especially religious, which influenced the rationalist worldview that Einstein developed throughout his life. From a young age, Einstein showed an insatiable curiosity about the natural world. However, his academic development was somewhat uneven; he was brilliant in mathematics and physics, but had difficulty with traditional education, as he did not fit into the mechanical learning that was prevalent in German schools at the time.

In 1896, Einstein entered the Zurich Polytechnic (today ETH Zurich), where he studied physics and mathematics. After graduating in 1900, he spent some years unable to find an academic position, which led him to work as a clerk at the Patent Office in Bern, Switzerland. This period proved to be one of the most productive of his life, as, while working there, he continued to independently research theoretical physics.

The year 1905, known as Einstein's annus mirabilis, marked the beginning of his rise to scientific stardom. During that year, he published four papers that radically transformed physics. The topics of these papers ranged from the photoelectric effect, and Brownian theory, to the special theory of relativity, culminating in the equation $E=mc^2$.

Photoelectric Effect: In this paper, Einstein proposed that light was composed of discrete particles (photons) and that these could free electrons from a metal when absorbed. This work laid the foundation for quantum theory, which earned him the Nobel Prize in Physics in 1921.

Brownian Motion: In another paper, Einstein explained how the random motion of particles suspended in a fluid (Brownian motion) was due to the impact of the fluid's molecules. This work provided key evidence for the existence of atoms, which at the time was not universally accepted.

Special Theory of Relativity: This was perhaps his most groundbreaking achievement that year. Einstein showed that the laws of physics are the same in all inertial reference frames and that the speed of light is constant, regardless of the observer's motion. This implied that space and time were not absolute, but relative to the observer's state of motion. This revolutionary idea radically changed physics and our understanding of the universe.

$E=mc^2$: In another 1905 paper, Einstein presented the equation that linked energy (E) to mass (m) via the speed of light squared (c^2). This equation demonstrated that mass and energy are interchangeable, a fundamental insight that would later be key in the development of nuclear power.

While the special theory of relativity solved problems related to inertial systems, Einstein realized that it did not address accelerated systems or gravity. For a decade, he worked on a more general theory that included gravity, and in 1915 he presented his general theory of relativity.

The general theory of relativity forever changed our understanding of gravity, which is not a direct force between two bodies, as Newton proposed, but the result of the curvature of space-time caused by the presence of mass and energy. According to this theory, large objects, such as planets and stars, warp space-time around them, explaining phenomena such as the orbit of planets and the bending of light around massive objects.

Empirical confirmation of the theory of general relativity came in 1919 when an expedition led by astronomer Arthur Eddington observed the shifting of light from distant stars as it passed close to the Sun during an eclipse. This discovery made Einstein a worldwide celebrity.

As his fame grew, so did his influence outside the scientific world. In the 1920s and 1930s, Einstein began to become increasingly involved in political and social issues. He was a convinced pacifist and a proponent of Zionism, although he believed in a peaceful solution for coexistence between Jews and Arabs in Palestine. However, his pacifist ideals were challenged with the rise of Nazism in Germany.

When Adolf Hitler came to power in 1933, Einstein, of Jewish origin, left Germany and went into exile in the United States. There he joined the Institute for Advanced Study in Princeton, where he would spend the rest of his life.

During World War II, Einstein took a more pragmatic stance regarding the use of force, especially upon learning of German advances in nuclear research. In 1939, he signed a famous letter to President Franklin D. Roosevelt, warning of the possibility that Germany was developing an atomic bomb. This letter influenced the creation of the Manhattan Project, although Einstein was never directly involved in it.

After the war, Einstein again became a strong advocate for nuclear disarmament and worked tirelessly for peace and civil rights, using his celebrity to promote these values.

Einstein's legacy in science is profound and multifaceted. His work on relativity forever changed theoretical physics, and many of his ideas were instrumental in the development of areas such as quantum physics, cosmology, and astrophysics. Some of the most influential areas of his work are highlighted below:

<u>Relativity:</u> Special and general relativity have been experimentally confirmed countless times and remain fundamental pillars in modern physics. Current experiments, such as those in GPS technology, rely on relativistic corrections to be accurate.

<u>Quantum physics:</u> Although Einstein had a complicated relationship with quantum physics, as he rejected the notion that the universe could be governed by chance ("God does not play dice"), his early work on the photoelectric effect was crucial to the development of this theory.

<u>Nuclear Energy:</u> The equation $E=mc^2$ provided the theoretical basis for understanding nuclear energy, leading to both civilian applications, such as nuclear power, and military developments, such as nuclear weapons.

Einstein not only influenced science, but his way of thinking also left a deep mark on 20th-century culture and philosophy. His insistence on the search for truth and his skepticism about chance in physics inspired generations of philosophers and thinkers to reflect on the nature of knowledge, reality, and the universe.

Einstein was also noted for his humility and humanism. Despite his worldwide fame, he was known for his simplicity and his rejection of honors and superficial recognition. In Einstein's words: "A man's worth should be seen in what he gives, not in what he can receive."

Einstein continued to work in science until the last days of his life, although he never achieved his goal of developing a unified field theory that reconciled gravity and electromagnetics in a single theoretical framework. He died on April 18, 1955, at the age of 76, in Princeton, New Jersey.

_____0_____

Other books by the author Phillips Tahuer that you will find on this platform:

• The greatest conspiracy theories

• Great robberies in history

• Famous murderers - the perverse side of the mind-

• Lives in captivity - Stories of real kidnappings-

• Agents, informants, and traitors - the world of espionage-

• Pirates of the 21st century

• Tragic loves

• 30 curiosities of World War II

• Dark experiments on humans

• Real-life heroes

• Powerful men in modern history

• Valentine's Day stories

• Practical Psychology Lessons